PORTFOLIOS
and
Other Assessments

Written by Julia Jasmine

Illustrated by Paula Spence

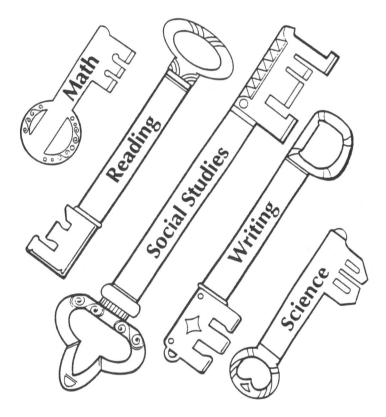

Teacher Created Materials, Inc.
P.O. Box 1040
Huntington Beach, CA 92647
©1993 Teacher Created Materials, Inc.
Made in U.S.A.

ISBN 1-55734-504-X

Table of Contents

Introduction

Assessment Is Changing

Assessment is changing both in theory and in practice before the very eyes and in the very classrooms of the teachers who are trying to implement it. In many cases the resulting demands made upon teachers by their school districts are both multiple and contradictory.

Teachers may be required to have students build portfolios and take performance tests while, at the same time, they must prepare these identical students for standardized multiple-choice, district-mandated tests and then report the various results on a single traditional, letter-grade report card. To top things off, these same districts may evaluate teachers on the basis of the test scores achieved by their students.

Much of this confused and overlapping effort in the area of assessment is caused by sincere philosophical differences among educators. Widely divergent blocks of opinion have tended to polarize thinking in educational circles in the United States as well as in England and other countries. One block is pushing for national standards, a national curriculum, and national testing. Another tends to individualize and leans toward performance assessment which is often seen as authentic assessment, although these two terms are not interchangeable. The issues are further confused by the fact that national testing could, in fact, be designed in the form of authentic performance assessment, and this is indeed the agenda of still another block.

So, we are not just rethinking assessment; we are rethinking our purpose. What do we really want for students? It is becoming more and more evident that what we know about learning is not supported by current educational practices. In many cases in the closing decade of the twentieth century we are teaching an eighteenth century curriculum in nineteenth century classrooms. The restructuring of our schools should address changes in curriculum and methodology as well as changes in methods of assessment.

This book is designed to help you make the leap into the new assessment. It explains the relationships between the types of performance assessments that are now being used and shows how they fit into your existing portfolio system. It gives you examples to look at, methods to try, tools to use, and forms to run off.

Portfolios and Other Assessments will prove to be a valuable addition to your existing teaching program.

Alternative Assessment

What Is Assessment?

Assessment is simply the systematic and purposeful use of various methods of looking at where you are and where you should be going. Ideally, any form of academic assessment will both inform students of their progress and help teachers identify what those students still need to learn. It will also provide information to the various publics served by the schools: parents, administrators, school boards, and taxpayers.

What Is Traditional Assessment?

The practices associated with traditional assessment consist of paper-and-pencil tests and usually focus on incremental skills that can be graded objectively. These tests are often multiple-choice and standardized, and they may be mandated by the district or the state. They have the advantage of being easily administered and easily graded. Their interpretation is not always easy, however, and the same results are often used to support opposing educational and/or political agendas.

What Is Alternative Assessment?

Alternative methods of assessment — sometimes referred to as the "new" assessment — are usually based on student performance and can be in the form of assigned tasks or can take place over a period of "real" time.

The assigned-tasks type of performance assessment may take the form of investigations, problem-solving situations, and assignments that combine reading and writing. Here, students can be asked to write to a prompt and are assessed on the basis of a familiar rubric. Or they can be given prescribed tasks that are then monitored by an observer with a checklist based on an appropriate task analysis.

The student performance that will be judged over a period of time may take the form of samples collected in — surprise! — a portfolio. In the absence of a district or school commitment or even in the face of a lack of interest, it is still good educational strategy to facilitate the students' use of portfolios. If the term frightens people (including you), you can call them "files." Portfolios in any subject area provide examples of work that serve not only as an assessment of performance over a period of time but can also be authentic, as long as they are not produced under artificial testing conditions. They should represent the ongoing work of the student for the year or for a part of the year.

Alternative Assessment *(cont.)*

Whether the performance is staged or occurs in real time, the tasks associated with alternative assessment will share some important, identifying characteristics: they will involve a group of learning behaviors; they will permit more than one solution; and they will result in a single product. In other words, to use the current educational catch-phrases, they will be complex, open-ended, and coherent.

In addition to assigned-task and student performance assessment, a third and less formal kind of performance assessment uses the teaching material to assess what has been taught. This kind of assessment, sometimes called Real-Life Assessment, recommends that teachers match their assessment tools to their teaching strategy. For example, if you want to assess comprehension, ask a student to retell the story he or she has just read. If you want to know if a student can predict, ask the student what will probably happen next.

Alternative methods of assessment are particularly appropriate for use in a classroom where thematic teaching is going on. Thematic teaching crosses the curriculum, adapts to various learning styles, stresses cooperative learning, provides flexible and adequate increments of time, and encourages the use of high level thinking skills. The assessment and evaluation of the learning that takes place in this kind of environment is much too complex for valid representation through the use of multiple-choice tests and letter grades alone.

How Does Portfolio Assessment Fit In?

Portfolio assessment can be thought of in two ways: as a container or a method.

The Portfolio as a Container

The portfolio as a container is simply a place to keep all the records generated by the new methods of assessment — the various drafts accumulated during the writing process along with their prompts and rubrics, the checklists that document the observations of assigned-task performance, and benchmark items such as end-of-unit tests in math and/or social studies.

The Portfolio as a Method

The portfolio used as a method may also contain the items listed above along with reading logs, anecdotal records, student/teacher contracts, and so on. But it is also used as a way to take a look at and compare work in order to observe progress over a period of time. The teacher, of course, looks at the work it contains for assessment purposes. More importantly, the student can look at the work and reflect on his or her own growth. In the course of this process the student participates in and claims ownership of the learning process. This is what makes portfolio assessment different from other forms of assessment. It is also what makes it worth all of the effort!

Alternative Assessment *(cont.)*

What If You Have To Do Everything?

Since alternative assessments based on performance are much more difficult to structure and evaluate than are traditional assessments, the teacher will do well to concentrate on the newer alternative forms of assessment and build in the skills and information that will be assessed in traditional ways.

The skills and concepts of standardized tests, multiple-choice or otherwise, can be covered very simply by obtaining a list of those skills and concepts and then imbedding them into the material to be taught during the semester or the year. This list of skills can usually be obtained from the material supplied by the publisher of the test and from the testing expert in a district. An example of this might involve short vowels in the primary grades. If you are teaching a literature-based reading program and you know your district's reading test includes a section on short vowels, concentrate on short-vowel words when you pull your spelling words from a literature selection or two.

The only other special, separate teaching that might be required to get students ready for tests of this kind is a review of some unique format that is not familiar to them and a brush-up in the skills that help in taking this kind of an objective test. If, for example, students have never taken a test based on multiple-choice questions, a practice test will help.

Miscellaneous Information

Testing experts are reminding us of some relevant facts and opinions (not always positive) about assessment:

- Different kinds of tests reflect different kinds of knowledge so we may want to assess in many different ways. We do not have to choose between types of assessment. We can have it all! (In many cases teachers feel as if we already have it all! Our students are tested more than any other students in the world.)

- Performance is knowledge in use. The testing tool must give evidence of the knowledge that has been acquired, and also show the competence and originality with which it is applied.

- Teachers will always focus on tests so the tests had better be good (well designed, high level, relevant to instruction), or instruction itself will suffer.

- As poor as some standardized tests are, teacher-made tests can be even worse. Both standardized and teacher-made tests are often written at the knowledge and recall levels of Bloom's taxonomy, and teacher-made tests tend to be narrow in their focus.

    Bloom's Taxonomy

    — Knowledge: Recalls facts and information.

    — Comprehension: Demonstrates basic understanding.

    — Application: Uses information in a new way.

    — Analysis: Examines parts in order to better understand the whole.

    — Synthesis: Puts parts together to form a new idea or product.

    — Evaluation: Forms opinions supported by sound reasoning.

Authentic Assessment

Just One Kind of Performance Assessment

Carol A. Meyer writes in the May, 1992 issue of *Educational Leadership* that we must be clear about the differences between authentic assessment and performance assessment if we are to support one another in developing improved assessment tools. A direct writing assessment in which students generate original writing samples under standardized conditions is a performance assessment, but it is not an authentic assessment because the context is contrived or staged. Papers chosen from a student's portfolio of work developed during the year constitute an assessment that is both a performance assessment and an authentic assessment because the writing was produced in a process more like that of real life and was — or should have been — reflected upon by the student. Meyer says that the significant factor in determining the authenticity of a writing assignment is that the focus of control remains with the student in areas such as choice of topic, time allocated, and writing conditions.

An example of this difference would look like this: You as a teacher want to assess your students' ability to write a persuasive letter. If you contrive a writing assignment in which you ask your students to write letters to the editor of a local newspaper that has published an article criticizing your school, you have created a tool for performance assessment. If you clip the article from the paper, bring it to class, and read it aloud with so much emotion that the students all say, "We will write a letter to that newspaper to persuade the editor that he/she is wrong," you have created a tool for authentic performance assessment.

These same criteria apply to performance assessments in other areas of the curriculum. For example, a science investigation that is dictated by a prompt may be a performance assessment, but it is not an authentic assessment. A science investigation that grows out of a student's interest, is developed as an individual (or group) project, and is documented by observations recorded with a system devised by the student (or students) would be both an authentic and a performance assessment.

None of this is meant to suggest in any way that there is anything wrong with a performance assessment that is not "authentic." An excellent teacher might wait for years — poised to perform an authentic assessment — before even one student developed a scientific or mathematical project based purely on individual and original interest. It is perfectly all right to stage a performance assessment — choosing a topic, allocating the time, and outlining the criteria for success. Just don't call it "authentic" in the purest meaning of the word.

(Interestingly enough, Grant Wiggins, the man who coined the term "authentic assessment," defined it as the performance of a task in a situation that most closely matches the standards and challenges of real life. According to him, it is up to educators to recreate this climate in the classroom.)

Assessment and Evaluation

What's the Difference?

Assessment and evaluation — these two words are often used interchangeably. However, for our purposes, we will use them to mean different things. Assessment, in this book, will mean the systematic and purposeful use of various methods of looking at student progress and achievement. Evaluation, on the other hand, will indicate the process of judging the assessment results for one purpose or another. If you assess a child's ability to solve a math problem in September and again in December, you can evaluate the progress he or she has made by comparing the two assessments.

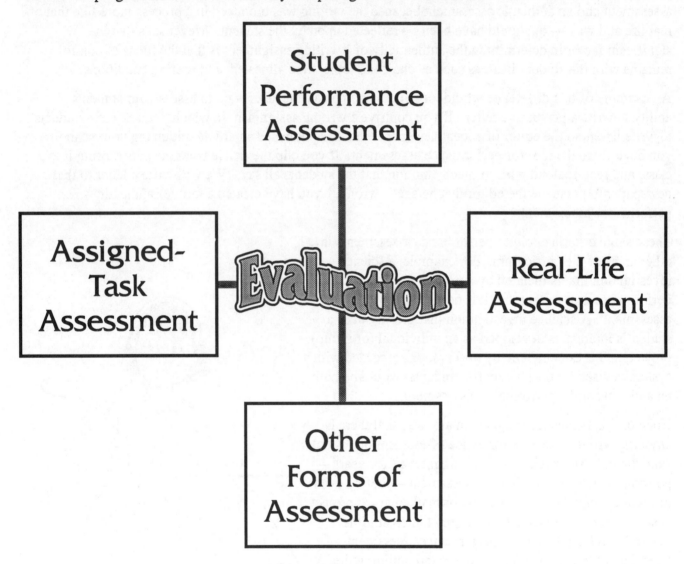

Using Portfolios for Assessment/Evaluation

Assessment using the portfolio method means gathering important information about the learning process over a period of time. Evaluation using the portfolio method means making some judgements about the amount and kind of progress shown by the collected samples and by the associated narrative comments (anecdotal records).

Rubric-Based Assessment: What, How, When, and Why

The 3 R's of Assessment

The "3 R's" of assessment are Rubrics, 'Riting, and 'Rithmetic. Both the products of the writing process along with the rubrics used to grade these products and samples of the new open-ended math along with the rubrics used to grade them are important parts of the new assessment and ready-made components of portfolio assessment. This is true whether you are thinking of the portfolio as a container or as a method. The written pieces and the math samples not only go into the portfolio but also lend themselves to the process of reflection which is one of the unique features of portfolio assessment.

What Is an Open-Ended Math Problem?

An open-ended math problem is a problem constructed in such a way that the student is encouraged to be creative in working toward a solution. The problem may have more than one potential solution and its purpose is to help the student clarify the thinking inherent in a math concept rather than reach some "right" answer. It may also involve a spin-off into other concepts or multiple applications of the original concept. The use of a rubric to grade open-ended math problems helps to keep the focus on how the student thought about the problem rather than what the answer turned out to be.

What Is a Rubric Anyway?

The word "rubric" literally means "rule." When the word is used in connection with assessment, a rubric is a scoring guide that differentiates, on an articulated scale, among a group of student samples that respond to the same prompt and range from the excellent response to one that is inappropriate and needs revision.

How Many Kinds of Rubrics Are There?

There are two types of rubrics: *holistic* and *analytic*.

A Holistic Rubric

- This rubric is used to measure the overall effect of a piece of writing (or any response to a prompt) with a set of appropriate guidelines. A holistic rubric is not quantitative.

An Analytic Rubric

- This rubric consists of score points assigned to various elements to be looked for in a written response. Analytic rubrics are totally quantitative.

Rubric-Based Assessment:
What, How, When, and Why *(cont.)*

Why Was the Holistic Rubric Developed?

Holistic and analytic rubrics can be used alone or can complement one another since they measure different things. The writing process is almost completely associated with the holistic rubric. It was developed at least in part in reaction to the use of the analytic rubric which tends to concentrate on the basic mechanical aspects of writing.

How Does the Holistic Rubric Promote Fluency?

One might say that holistic scoring rubrics came in with the writing process. They were part of the attempt to improve student writing. The holistic approach was particularly designed to promote fluency.

Up to that time the use of analytic rubrics had encouraged students to write as little as possible since their errors in mechanics were being counted against them and the more sentences, the more chance of errors. Students being assessed with an analytic rubric could pass a proficiency test by writing one topic sentence and four short, simple (but neither fragmented nor run-on) supporting sentences. They might fail the same test by expanding on their ideas and inadvertently including a fragment or a run-on sentence or more than two or three spelling errors.

A well-developed holistic rubric prevents this from happening by focusing attention on organization, the expression of ideas, and the use of lively language.

Where Do Rubrics Come From?

Rubrics are developed by people who are making and scoring student samples of one kind or another. These people might be writers for publishing companies, district test coordinators, or classroom teachers. The best rubrics are carefully designed to assess the desired skills and to go with the samples they will measure.

Sometimes the entire staff of a school will meet together to develop sequential rubrics that will meet the needs of teachers and kids in all the grades. This kind of articulation across grade levels, of course, encourages students to make smooth transitions from grade to grade. (See Do-It-Yourself Directions on page 51.)

Rubrics are basically used in two ways: traditionally as an assessment device and more recently as a teaching tool.

Rubric-Based Assessment: What, How, When, and Why *(cont.)*

How Are Rubrics Used in Assessment?

If a school district uses a writing sample to judge student progress at certain "check point" grade levels, a group of teachers from that district often meets together to score these writing samples using a rubric developed by the district.

Very often, someone has pre-screened the papers, finding examples of excellent, average, and poor writing samples. These examples (with the names of students and schools deleted) are run off and, together with copies of the appropriate rubrics, made into packets for the teachers who are to be scoring the papers. If there are twenty papers in each packet, the teachers may be asked to read the first five and score them according to the rubric. After this has been done, scores are compared and discussed until enough agreement has been reached to ensure a start toward consistency. This process is repeated for all of the papers in the packet. The rest of the papers are then read and scored, each one by at least two readers. If the scores agree, that score is official. If the scores disagree, a third reader decides. This process is repeated during the day, bringing the group together with a smaller packet to maintain consistency in scoring.

Unless district testing has been structured to lead the students being tested through all the steps in the writing process, scorers must keep in mind that they are really reading a first-draft composition and structure their standards accordingly.

It has been found, interestingly enough, that even though the eventual results of this kind of assessment are really PASS/FAIL, more valid scoring is obtained by having at least four scores:

Excellent or High Pass (3)	Average or Pass (2)	Low or No Pass (1)	No Response (0)

If the choice is simply Pass or Fail, the few papers that are really excellent and off the scale on the top skew the results and make the scorers too critical of papers that are really Average or Pass.

This same process, modified to suit the situation, can be used within a school. Teachers on the same grade level often read the papers from one another's classes after discussing the rubric they are using. In the case of classroom scoring, papers that might be called Low or Fail in more formal situations are referred to as Needs Revision or Needs Correction. Also, the standards can be adjusted to a higher level since classroom papers should have been allowed to go through the whole writing process of drafts, editing, and revision.

This same process is also used to grade open-ended math questions. The rubric, however, is often modified or even built by the scoring team as they read the students' papers. They convene and re-convene, changing and redesigning their scoring tool to accommodate the thinking of the students being tested.

Rubric-Based Assessment: What, How, When, and Why *(cont.)*

How Are Rubrics Used as Teaching Tools?

Once upon a time rubrics were secret documents hidden away by the teacher or by the district testing office and brought out only to grade the writing samples that determined whether a student would pass or fail or even graduate. Today, rubrics are shared with and even developed by students as part of the writing process. A student who is generating a writing sample should have free access to the standards by which the finished work will be judged. The rubric can, in fact, be attached to the series of drafts that makes up a writing process assignment and included with it in the student's portfolio.

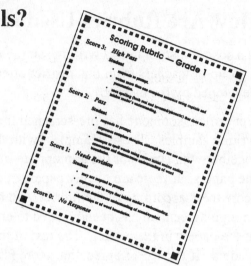

Are Samples Available?

On the pages that follow you will find sample prompts and scripts for 1st through 6th grade writing samples, the rubrics that go with them, and sets of student writing samples representing a range of achievement based on those prompts and rubrics. You will also find a DO-IT-YOURSELF set consisting of a blank teacher script, student writing sample form, and scoring rubric. These are ready for you to use to create assessment tools of your own.

Following those pages, you will find a generalized task rubric that can be used for any subject area. It is followed by prompts and elaborated rubrics for open-ended math problems across the grade levels together with a range of samples.

We finish up this section with some "Summary of Progress" forms to help you keep records that will let you see at a glance the work of one student or the relative progress of a whole class.

A Quick Review of the Writing Process Itself

If you use the writing process every day, week in and week out, feel free to move right along to RUBRICS IN ACTION (page 14). If, on the other hand, you would like a refresher in the writing process, turn to page 13 for a quick review.

What Is the Writing Process?

The "Real Life" Approach

The writing process is the "real life" approach to teaching students how to write. It replicates the way people really use writing daily as a life skill and a creative tool.

People who "really" write first have a need to write, either practical or creative. They make notes as ideas occur to them. They may have an intensive private brainstorming session to start their process. They look at their notes or brainstormed list. They choose, prioritize, and organize them. They put their first draft on paper. If they have time, they may put this draft away for some time to take a fresh look at it later. Then they edit. They may ask someone to proof their work. Only after all of this does the "real" writer attempt a final draft. Even this draft may need more revision, perhaps for clarity or the addition of concrete examples.

The Steps in Teaching the Writing Process

Using the "writing process" in the classroom is an attempt to use the steps outlined above to make writing real to students. First, the student is presented with a reason to write. This can be a discussion, a visual experience, a reading selection, and so on. An individual or class brainstorm session follows. Students are then allowed to reorganize their ideas. They may be comfortable with outlining or clustering. It is nice to give them more than one organizational technique. At this point, the students write their first drafts. They should be encouraged to get their ideas on paper without undue concern for the mechanics of writing.

The editing process follows the first draft and may result in multiple drafts. There can be peer-editing, self-editing, teacher-editing, editing for spelling and mechanics, and/or editing for clarity and style. These parts of the process lend themselves to exercises in cooperative learning and to the use of the computer for word processing. If students are using a computer, they should print each successive draft for optimum practice in tracing the growth of a piece of writing. These successive drafts are ideal for portfolio assessment.

It Is Different from the Traditional Method

This process differs from the traditional method of teaching writing in three notable ways. First, the writing process can stop at any point. The students or the teacher can say, "I've gotten what I need from this piece. I'll leave it at this point." Second, students are not expected to produce "perfect" examples of their writing for grading purposes when what they are really doing is producing a first draft essay for which they had no time to prepare. Third, students are encouraged to learn that writing is a process and to be patient with themselves, to stretch their skills, and to take pride in improving their own work.

Rubrics in Action

Sectional Table of Contents

Suggestion to the Teacher: The script on this page and the writing sample form (page 16) and rubric (page 17) were used to generate the examples of 1st grade writing that follow. Run off enough writing sample forms for your class and use this script to generate your own set of writing samples. Then use the rubric to grade them. To use for portfolio assessment purposes, staple a set together for each of your students — include writing sample, script, and rubric — and place in their portfolios.

Prompt for a Writing Sample — Grade 1
Teacher Script

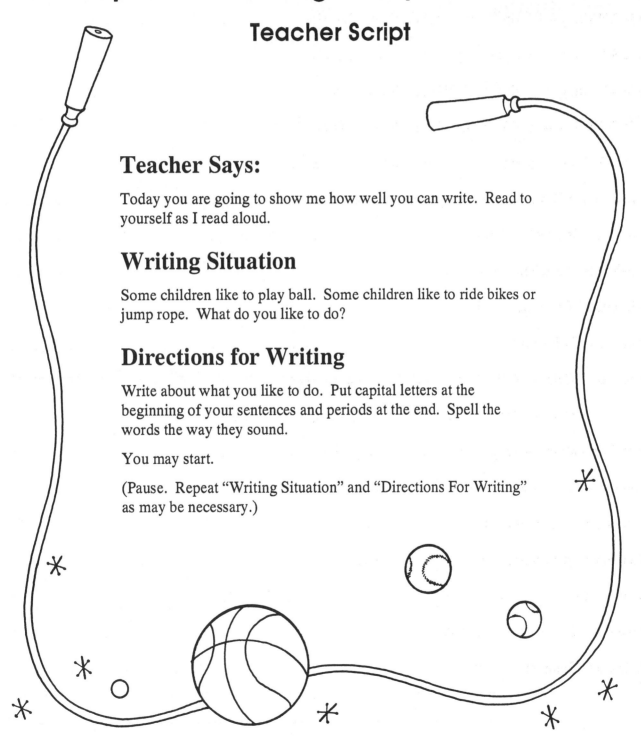

Teacher Says:

Today you are going to show me how well you can write. Read to yourself as I read aloud.

Writing Situation

Some children like to play ball. Some children like to ride bikes or jump rope. What do you like to do?

Directions for Writing

Write about what you like to do. Put capital letters at the beginning of your sentences and periods at the end. Spell the words the way they sound.

You may start.

(Pause. Repeat "Writing Situation" and "Directions For Writing" as may be necessary.)

Prompt for a Writing Sample — Grade 1
Student Writing Sample

Name _____   Date _____

Writing Situation

Some children like to play ball. Some children like to ride bikes or jump rope. What do you like to do?

Directions for Writing

Write about what you like to do. Put capital letters at the beginning of your sentences and periods at the end. Spell the words the way they sound.

_____

- -

_____

_____

- -

_____

_____

- -

_____

_____

- -

_____

_____

- -

_____

Scoring Rubric — Grade 1

Score 3: *High Pass*

Student

- responds to prompt.
- writes more than one complete sentence using capitals and punctuation.
- uses spelling (both real and invented/phonetic) that does not inhibit reader's understanding.

Score 2: *Pass*

Student

- responds to prompt.
- expresses complete thoughts, although may not use standard sentences.
- attempts to spell words using correct initial and/or ending consonants and demonstrates understanding of word boundaries.

Score 1: *Needs Revision*

Student

- may not respond to prompt.
- expresses self in ways that inhibit reader's understanding.
- does not demonstrate understanding of sound/symbol relationships or of word boundaries.

Score 0: *No Response*

*At 1st grade level, Needs Revision really means "needs more time to learn skills," "needs additional maturity," etc.

(The papers that follow have been graded according to this rubric and can serve as "checkpoints" for grading papers at this grade level.)

Prompt for a Writing Sample — Grade 1

(3)

Student Writing Sample

Name __Brett__   Date __Feb. 23__

Writing Situation

Some children like to play ball. Some children like to ride bikes or jump rope. What do you like to do?

Directions for Writing

Write about what you like to do. Put capital letters at the beginning of your sentences and periods at the end. Spell the words the way they sound.

I like to play ball. I like to play jump rope.

Prompt for a Writing Sample — Grade 1

Student Writing Sample

Name Mike

Date March 21

Writing Situation

Some children like to play ball. Some children like to ride bikes or jump rope. What do you like to do?

Directions for Writing

Write about what you like to do. Put capital letters at the beginning of your sentences and periods at the end. Spell the words the way they sound.

I like to Play
socker weth my
frnds my frnds like
to Play weth my.

Prompt for a Writing Sample — Grade 1

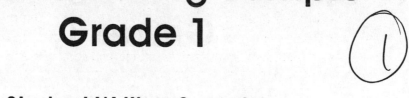

Student Writing Sample

Name **Kelly**   Date **Dec. 20**

Writing Situation

Some children like to play ball. Some children like to ride bikes or jump rope. What do you like to do?

Directions for Writing

Write about what you like to do. Put capital letters at the beginning of your sentences and periods at the end. Spell the words the way they sound.

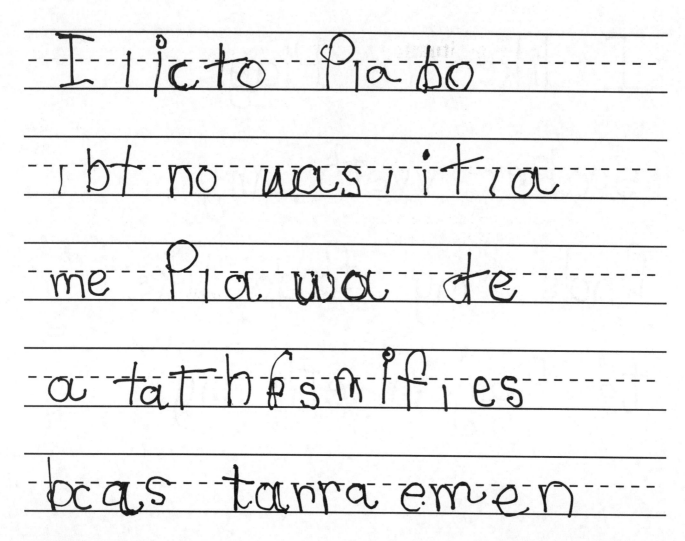

I lieto Piabo
rbt no was itia
me Pia wa te
a tat hEsnifies
bcas tarra emen

Suggestion to the Teacher: The script on this page and the writing sample form (page 22) and rubric (page 23) were used to generate the examples of second grade writing that follow. Run off enough writing sample forms for your class and use this script to generate your own set of writing samples. Then use the rubric to grade them. To use for portfolio assessment purposes, staple a set together for each of your students — include writing sample, script, and rubric — and place in their portfolios.

- -

Prompt for a Writing Sample — Grade 2
Teacher Script

Teacher Says:

Today you are going to show me how well you can write. Read to yourself as I read aloud.

Writing Situation

Winter is coming. In some places the weather gets colder and colder. Does it get cold where you live? What do you like best about winter?

Directions for Writing

Write about winter. Tell about the weather. Tell what you like best about winter. Use correct capitals and periods. Spell the words the way they sound.

You may start.

(Pause. Repeat "Writing Situation" and "Directions For Writing" as may be necessary.)

See "Suggestions to the Teacher" on page 21.

Prompt for a Writing Sample — Grade 2

Student Writing Sample

Name _____   Date _____

Writing Situation

Winter is coming. In some places the weather gets colder and colder. Does it get cold where you live? What do you like best about winter?

Directions for Writing

Write about winter. Tell about the weather. Tell what you like best about winter. Use correct capitals and periods. Spell the words the way they sound.

_____

- -

_____

_____

- -

_____

_____

- -

_____

_____

- -

_____

_____

- -

_____

Scoring Rubric — Grade 2

Score 3: *High Pass*

Student

- responds to prompt.
- writes several sentences using capitals and ending punctuation.
- uses spelling (both real and invented/phonetic) that does not inhibit reader's understanding.

Score 2: *Pass*

Student

- responds to prompt.
- expresses complete thoughts although sentences may be fragments or run on.
- uses spelling (both real and invented/phonetic) that, for the most part, does not inhibit the reader's understanding.

Score 1: *Needs Revision*

Student

- may not respond to prompt.
- expresses self in ways that inhibit reader's understanding.
- does not demonstrate understanding of sound/symbol relationships or of word boundaries.

Score 0: *No Response*

(The papers that follow have been graded according to this rubric and can serve as "checkpoints" for grading papers at this level.)

Prompt for a Writing Sample — Grade 2

Student Writing Sample

Name **Juan**

Date **11/16/92**

③

Writing Situation

Winter is coming. In some places the weather gets colder and colder. Does it get colder where you live? What do you like best about winter?

Directions for Writing

Write about winter. Tell about the weather. Tell what you like best about winter. Use capitals and periods. Spell the words the way they sound.

Winter is very, very cold. I go skiing in the winter. Sometimes I make a snowman. It snows a lot in the winter.

Prompt for a Writing Sample — Grade 2

Student Writing Sample

2+

Name Tessa

Date Nov. 16, 1992

Writing Situation

Winter is coming. In some places the weather gets colder and colder. Does it get cold where you live? What do you like best about winter?

Directions for Writing

Write about winter. Tell about the weather. Tell what you like best about winter. Use capitals and periods. Spell the words the way they sound.

Because of Cremes
and sonw camp. Cremes
Eve is when my mom got
miard. The weather
gets cold.

Prompt for a Writing Sample — Grade 2

Student Writing Sample

Name **Larry**   Date **11-16-92**

①

Writing Situation

Winter is coming. In some places the weather gets colder and colder. Does it get cold where you live? What do you like best about winter?

Directions for Writing

Write about winter. Tell about the weather. Tell what you like best about winter. Use capitals and periods. Spell the words the way they sound.

I Like play wet my ball

Today is farrny day I am

happy day I am go

to the stor today my

mather i happy

Suggestion to the Teacher: The directions on this page and the writing sample form (page 28) and rubric (page 29) were used to generate the examples of 3rd grade writing that follow. Run off enough Writing Sample Forms for your class and use them to generate your own set of writing samples. Then use the rubric to grade them. To use for portfolio assessment purposes, staple a set together for each of your students — include both the writing sample and the rubric — and place in their portfolios.

Prompt for a Writing Sample — Grade 3

Teacher Script

Teacher Says:

Today you are going to show me how well you can write.

Read the Writing Situation and the Directions for Writing to yourself as I read them aloud. Then write your piece on the lines provided.

Writing Situation

Everybody has a favorite food. Some people like spicy foods such as pizza and spaghetti. Other people like sweet foods such as ice cream or chocolate brownies.

Directions for Writing

Write a description of your favorite food. Try to tell about it in such a way that the reader can almost see it, smell it, and taste it. Use correct capitals and end punctuation. If you are not sure how to spell a word, spell it the way it sounds.

You may start.

Prompt for a Writing Sample — Grade 3

Student Writing Sample

Name _____   Date _____

Writing Situation

Everybody has a favorite food. Some people like spicy foods such as pizza and spaghetti. Other people like sweet foods such as ice cream or chocolate brownies.

Directions for Writing

Write a description of your favorite food. Try to tell about it in such a way that the reader can almost see it, smell it, and taste it. Use correct capitals and end punctuation. If you are not sure how to spell a word, spell it the way it sounds.

_____

_____

_____

_____

_____

_____

_____

_____

_____

_____

_____

_____

_____

_____

_____

See "Suggestion to the Teacher" on page 27.

Scoring Rubric — Grade 3

Score 3: *High Pass*

Student

- responds to prompt.
- uses vivid descriptive language that appeals to the senses of sight, smell, and taste.
- writes enough to adequately address the topic.
- uses correct capitals and ending punctuation.
- uses spelling (both real and invented/phonetic) that does not inhibit reader's understanding.

Score 2: *Pass*

Student

- responds to prompt.
- uses language that appeals to at least one sense.
- expresses complete thoughts although sentences may be fragments or run-ons and may not always be correctly capitalized and/or punctuated.
- uses spelling (both real and invented/phonetic) that, for the most part, does not inhibit the reader's understanding.

Score 1: *Needs Revision*

Student

- may not respond to prompt.
- does not use language that appeals to the senses.
- expresses self in ways that inhibit reader's understanding.
- does not demonstrate understanding of relationship between capitalization/punctuation and sentence structure.
- does not demonstrate understanding of sound/symbol relationships in spelling.

Score 0: *No Response*

(The papers that follow have been graded according to this rubric and can serve as "checkpoints" for grading papers at this level.)

See "Suggestion to the Teacher" on page 27.

Prompt for a Writing Sample — Grade 3

Student Writing Sample

2+ /B-

Name _Pham_   Date _Nov. 25, 1992_

Writing Situation

Everybody has a favorite food. Some people like spicy foods such as pizza and spaghetti. Other people like sweet foods such as ice cream or chocolate brownies.

Directions for Writing

Write a description of your favorite food. Try to tell about it in such a way that the reader can almost see it, smell it, and taste it. Use correct capitals and end punctuation. If you are not sure how to spell a word, spell it the way it sounds.

My favrot food is makeruny
and cheese. It is shapet like
a circle. It tastes like
spegede. It very chooy. It is
tasty and yumy. And I love
the cheese.

Prompt for a Writing Sample — Grade 3

Student Writing Sample ②

Name __Maria__   Date __Nov. 25, 1992__

Writing Situation

Everybody has a favorite food. Some people like spicy foods such as pizza and spaghetti. Other people like sweet foods such as ice cream or chocolate brownies.

Directions for Writing

Write a description of your favorite food. Try to tell about it in such a way that the reader can almost see it, smell it, and taste it. Use correct capitals and end punctuation. If you are not sure how to spell a word, spell it the way it sounds.

My favorite food is browneys
soft and sqoshy. They have hard
soft topping with sprinkls.
Chalklet chips in it to. Chalklet
milk with it would be good To.

Prompt for a Writing Sample — Grade 3

Student Writing Sample

(It)

Name __Trent__   Date __Nov 25, 1992__

Writing Situation

Everybody has a favorite food. Some people like spicy foods such as pizza and spaghetti. Other people like sweet foods such as ice cream or chocolate brownies.

Directions for Writing

Write a description of your favorite food. Try to tell about it in such a way that the reader can almost see it, smell it, and taste it. Use correct capitals and end punctuation. If you are not sure how to spell a word, spell it the way it sounds.

Favrate
food is pizze. It has red and sace sars.
It has lrost of cheese and cheese and
cheese......... It sais like cheese
and bread and sars. When you put
it in your mathy you tocaks the cheese
and bread and sars.

Suggestion to the Teacher: The directions on this page and the writing sample form (page 34) and rubric (page 35) were used to generate the examples of 4th grade writing that follow. Run off enough Writing Sample Forms for your class and use them to generate your own set of writing samples. Then use the rubric to grade them. To use for portfolio assessment purposes, staple a set together for each of your students — include both the writing sample and the rubric — and place in their portfolios.

Prompt for a Writing Sample — Grade 4

Teacher Script

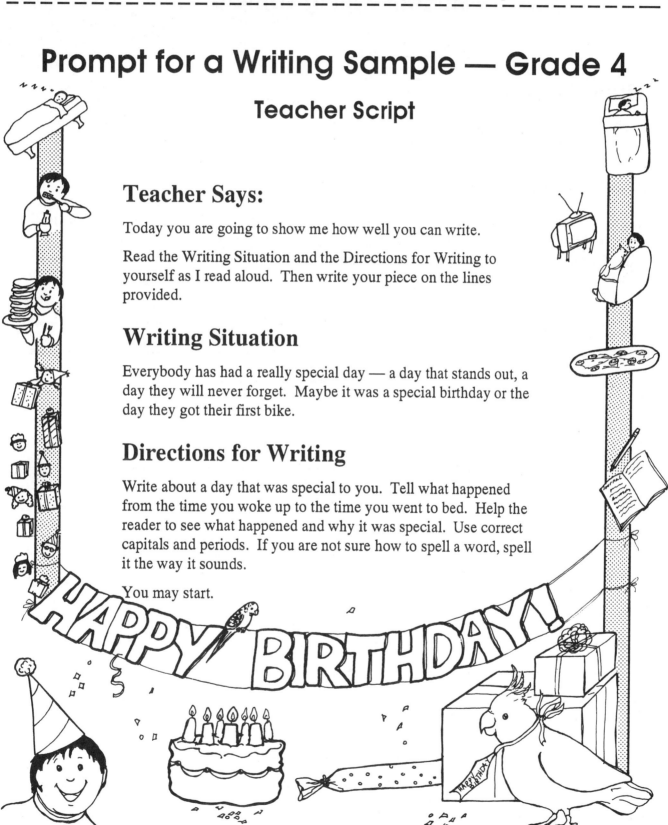

Teacher Says:

Today you are going to show me how well you can write.

Read the Writing Situation and the Directions for Writing to yourself as I read aloud. Then write your piece on the lines provided.

Writing Situation

Everybody has had a really special day — a day that stands out, a day they will never forget. Maybe it was a special birthday or the day they got their first bike.

Directions for Writing

Write about a day that was special to you. Tell what happened from the time you woke up to the time you went to bed. Help the reader to see what happened and why it was special. Use correct capitals and periods. If you are not sure how to spell a word, spell it the way it sounds.

You may start.

Prompt for a Writing Sample — Grade 4

Student Writing Sample

Name _____   Date _____

Writing Situation

Everybody has had a really special day — a day that stands out, a day they will never forget. Maybe it was a special birthday or the day they got their first bike.

Directions for Writing

Write about a day that was special to you. Tell what happened from the time you woke up to the time you went to bed. Help the reader to see what happened and why it was special. Use correct capitals and periods. If you are not sure how to spell a word, spell it the way it sounds.

_____

_____

_____

_____

_____

_____

_____

_____

_____

_____

_____

_____

_____

_____

_____

_____

See "Suggestion to the Teacher" on page 33.

Scoring Rubric — Grade 4

Score 3: *High Pass*

Student

- responds to prompt.
- narrates day's events in chronological order.
- addresses the idea of cause/effect.
- writes enough to adequately address the topic.
- uses correct capitals and ending punctuation.
- uses spelling (both real and invented/phonetic) that does not inhibit reader's understanding.

Score 2: *Pass*

Student

- responds to prompt.
- may not tell events in chronological order.
- may not relate cause and effect clearly.
- expresses complete thoughts, although sentences may not be correctly capitalized and/or punctuated.
- uses spelling (both real and invented/phonetic) that, for the most part, does not inhibit the reader's understanding.

Score 1: *Needs Revision*

Student

- may not respond to prompt.
- does not tell about the events of the day.
- does not attempt to tell why the day was special.
- expresses self in ways that inhibit reader's understanding.
- does not demonstrate understanding of relationship between capitalization/punctuation and sentence structure.
- does not demonstrate understanding of sound/symbol relationships in spelling.

Score 0: *No Response*

(The papers that follow have been graded according to this rubric and can serve as "checkpoints" for grading papers at this level.)

Prompt for a Writing Sample — Grade 4

Student Writing Sample

③

Name _Jennifer_   Date _Nov. 25, 1992_

Writing Situation

Everybody has had a really special day — a day that stands out, a day they will never forget. Maybe it was a special birthday or the day they got their first bike.

Directions for Writing

Write about a day that was special to you. Tell what happened from the time you woke up to the time you went to bed. Help the reader to see what happened and why it was special. Use correct capitals and periods. If you are not sure how to spell a word, spell it the way it sounds.

I woke up and knew today would be special. Today I would pick up my puppy. I qickly got dressed, ate breakfast and got in the car. C'mon! Hurry! My mom, dad and my brother got in the car. We drove to my dads' friends house. We rang the door bell. She let us in I saw jenny the puppy's mother. I went over to the play pen and looked at the puppy's. Then I saw him. A puppy with a green ribbon. We took him home. His name is Indy.

See "Suggestion to the Teacher" on page 33.

Prompt for a Writing Sample — Grade 4

Student Writing Sample

(2+)

Name _Mischa_   Date _11-25-92_

Writing Situation

Everybody has had a really special day — a day that stands out, a day they will never forget. Maybe it was a special birthday or the day they got their first bike.

Directions for Writing

Write about a day that was special to you. Tell what happened from the time you woke up to the time you went to bed. Help the reader to see what happened and why it was special. Use correct capitals and periods. If you are not sure how to spell a word, spell it the way it sounds.

The special day of mine was
when it was my birthday.
I got lots of preasents, I had
my friends Ever. I couldn't
think about any thing else.
It was very fun on my birthday
we got to play games.
that was, my special day
I couldn't even sleep.

Prompt for a Writing Sample — Grade 4

Student Writing Sample

(1)

Name *Loan*

Date 11-25-92

Writing Situation

Everybody has had a really special day — a day that stands out, a day they will never forget. Maybe it was a special birthday or the day they got their first bike.

Directions for Writing

Write about a day that was special to you. Tell what happened from the time you woke up to the time you went to bed. Help the reader to see what happened and why it was special. Use correct capitals and periods. If you are not sure how to spell a word, spell it the way it sounds.

I liked the time I whent water skeing

Suggestion to the Teacher: The directions on this page and the writing sample form (page 40) and rubric (page 41) on the next two pages were used to generate the examples of 5th grade writing that follow. Run off enough Writing Sample Forms for your class and use them to generate your own set of writing samples. Then use the rubric to grade them. To use for portfolio assessment purposes, staple a set together for each of your students — include both the writing sample and the rubric — and place in their portfolios.

- -

Prompt for a Writing Sample — Grade 5

Teacher Script

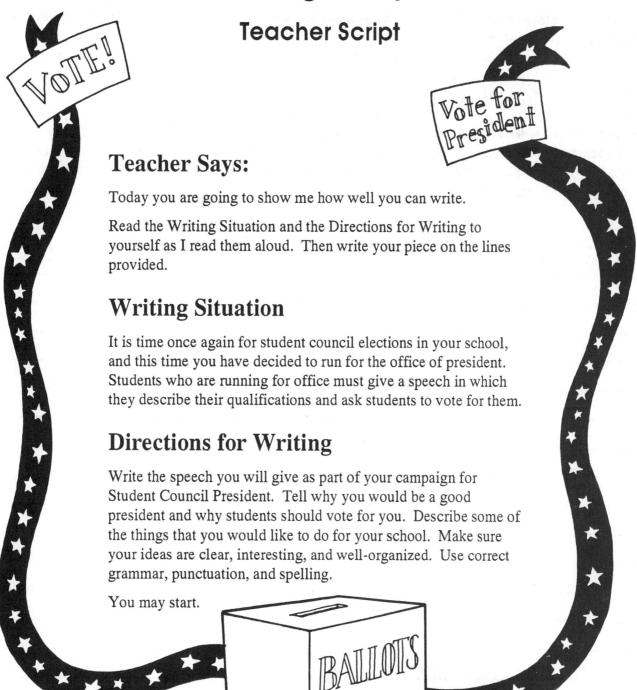

Teacher Says:

Today you are going to show me how well you can write.

Read the Writing Situation and the Directions for Writing to yourself as I read them aloud. Then write your piece on the lines provided.

Writing Situation

It is time once again for student council elections in your school, and this time you have decided to run for the office of president. Students who are running for office must give a speech in which they describe their qualifications and ask students to vote for them.

Directions for Writing

Write the speech you will give as part of your campaign for Student Council President. Tell why you would be a good president and why students should vote for you. Describe some of the things that you would like to do for your school. Make sure your ideas are clear, interesting, and well-organized. Use correct grammar, punctuation, and spelling.

You may start.

See "Suggestion to the Teacher" on page 39.

Prompt for a Writing Sample — Grade 5

Student Writing Sample

Name _____   Date _____

Writing Situation

It is time once again for student council elections in your school, and this time you have decided to run for the office of president. Students who are running for office must give a speech in which they describe their qualifications and ask students to vote for them.

Directions for Writing

Write the speech you will give as part of your campaign for Student Council President. Tell why you would be a good president and why students should vote for you. Describe some of the things that you would like to do for your school. Make sure your ideas are clear, interesting, and well-organized. Use correct grammar, punctuation, and spelling.

_____

_____

_____

_____

_____

_____

_____

_____

_____

_____

_____

_____

_____

_____

_____

See "Suggestion to the Teacher" on page 39.

Scoring Rubric — Grade 5

Score 3: *High Pass*

Student

- responds to prompt.

- demonstrates noticeable evidence of organizational skills (e.g., strong opening and conclusion).

- demonstrates mastery of conventions (grammar, usage, mechanics, spelling).

- expresses interesting ideas; uses lively language.

Score 2: *Pass*

Student

- responds to prompt.

- demonstrates adequate evidence of organizational skills (e.g., opening and conclusion).

- demonstrates use of conventions that do not inhibit reader's understanding.

- demonstrates understanding of language through use of appropriate vocabulary.

Score 1: *Needs Revision*

Student

- may not respond to prompt.

- demonstrates little or no ability to organize material.

- does not use conventions correctly; reader's understanding is inhibited.

- uses inappropriate vocabulary.

Score 0: *No Response*

(The papers that follow have been graded according to this rubric and can serve as "checkpoints" for grading papers at this level.)

See "Suggestion to the Teacher" on page 39.

Prompt for a Writing Sample — Grade 5

Student Writing Sample ③

Name **Ian Roberts**   Date **Nov. 24, 1993**

Writing Situation

It is time once again for student council elections in your school, and this time you have decided to run for the office of president. Students who are running for office must give a speech in which they describe their qualifications and ask students to vote for them.

Directions for Writing

Write the speech you will give as part of your campaign for Student Council President. Tell why you would be a good president and why students should vote for you. Describe some of the things that you would like to do for your school. Make sure your ideas are clear, interesting, and well-organized. Use correct grammar, punctuation, and spelling.

Mrs. Duncan, ladies and gentlemen, boys and girls, my name is Ian Roberts and I'm running for your school president. The president needs intelligence, will power, and has to be able to make the right choice. Let me tell you about myself, I'm a straight A student, and I have been your fourth grade cabinet and Vice President. I wish I could promise things like soda machines, video games and things like that at school, but I can't, but I can do everything in my power to give Jefferson students the education and happiness they deserve.

See "Suggestion to the Teacher" on page 39.

Prompt for a Writing Sample — Grade 5

Student Writing Sample ②

Name Dirk Brown   Date Nov. 24, '92

Writing Situation

It is time once again for student council elections in your school and this time you have decided to run for the office of president. Students who are running for office must give a speech in which they describe their qualifications and ask students to vote for them.

Directions for Writing

Write the speech you will give as part of your campaign for Student Council President. Tell why you would be a good president and why students should vote for you. Describe some of the things that you would like to do for your school. Make sure your ideas are clear, interesting, and well-organized. Use correct grammar, punctuation, and spelling.

Staff mumebers students its time to make a new beging, to elect a new school president. Now one of the reasan I want your vote is beacause I beileve with hard work and effert we could make our school the best that it could be. One of the things we could do is have a student store or a pencil machine. These are only two of my ideas so please vote for me thank you.

See "Suggestion to the Teacher" on page 39.

Prompt for a Writing Sample — Grade 5

Student Writing Sample

Name *Marissa McKinley*　　　　Date *Nov. 24, '92*

Writing Situation

It is time once again for student council elections in your school, and this time you have decided to run for the office of president. Students who are running for office must give a speech in which they describe their qualifications and ask students to vote for them.

Directions for Writing

Write the speech you will give as part of your campaign for Student Council President. Tell why you would be a good president and why students should vote for you. Describe some of the things that you would like to do for your school. Make sure your ideas are clear, interesting, and well-organized. Use correct grammar, punctuation, and spelling.

Hi! am Marissa McKinley a lik to be a pet president beas is good. and a like and in the school. I have to vote for me an goind do put of the trahkend and life end oder vote for me Marissa.

Suggestion to the Teacher: The directions on this page and the writing sample form (page 46) and rubric (page 47) on the next two pages were used to generate the examples of 6th grade writing that follow. Run off enough Writing Sample Forms for your class and use them to generate your own set of writing samples. Then use the rubric to grade them. To use for portfolio assessment purposes, staple a set together for each of your students — include both the writing sample and the rubric — and place in their portfolios.

Prompt for a Writing Sample — Grade 6

Teacher Script

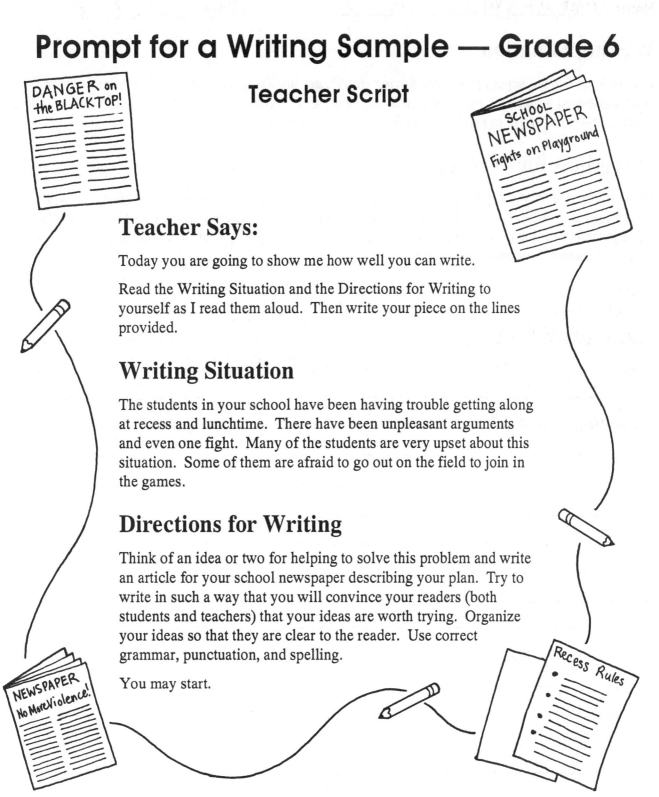

Teacher Says:

Today you are going to show me how well you can write.

Read the Writing Situation and the Directions for Writing to yourself as I read them aloud. Then write your piece on the lines provided.

Writing Situation

The students in your school have been having trouble getting along at recess and lunchtime. There have been unpleasant arguments and even one fight. Many of the students are very upset about this situation. Some of them are afraid to go out on the field to join in the games.

Directions for Writing

Think of an idea or two for helping to solve this problem and write an article for your school newspaper describing your plan. Try to write in such a way that you will convince your readers (both students and teachers) that your ideas are worth trying. Organize your ideas so that they are clear to the reader. Use correct grammar, punctuation, and spelling.

You may start.

See "Suggestion to the Teacher" on page 45.

Prompt for a Writing Sample — Grade 6

Student Writing Sample

Name _____   Date _____

Writing Situation

The students in your school have been having trouble getting along at recess and lunchtime. There have been unpleasant arguments and even one fight. Many of the students are very upset about this situation. Some of them are afraid to go out on the field to join in the games.

Directions for Writing

Think of an idea or two for helping to solve this problem and write an article for your school newspaper describing your plan. Try to write in such a way that you will convince your readers (both students and teachers) that your ideas are worth trying. Organize your ideas so that they are clear to the reader. Use correct grammar, punctuation, and spelling.

_____

_____

_____

_____

_____

_____

_____

_____

_____

_____

_____

_____

_____

_____

_____

_____

See "Suggestion to the Teacher" on page 45.

Scoring Rubric — Grade 6

Score 3: *High Pass*

Student

- responds to prompt.
- demonstrates noticeable evidence of organizational skills (e.g., strong opening and conclusion, appropriate paragraphing).
- demonstrates mastery of conventions (grammar, usage, mechanics, spelling).
- expresses interesting ideas; uses lively language.

Score 2: *Pass*

Student

- responds to prompt.
- demonstrates adequate evidence of organizational skills (e.g., opening and conclusion).
- demonstrates use of conventions that do not inhibit reader's understanding.
- demonstrates understanding of language through use of appropriate vocabulary.

Score 1: *Needs Revision*

Student

- may not respond to prompt.
- demonstrates little or no ability to organize material.
- does not use conventions correctly; reader's understanding is inhibited.
- uses inappropriate vocabulary.

Score 0: *No Response*

(The papers that follow have been graded according to this rubric and can serve as "checkpoints" for grading papers at this level.)

Prompt for a Writing Sample — Grade 6

Student Writing Sample ③

Name _Connie Lin_   Date _11-25-92_

Writing Situation

The students in your school have been having trouble getting along at recess and lunchtime. There have been unpleasant arguments and even one fight. Many of the students are very upset about this situation. Some of them are afraid to go out on the field to join in the games.

Directions for Writing

Think of an idea or two for helping to solve this problem and write an article for your school newspaper describing your plan. Try to write in such a way that you will convince your readers (both students and teachers) that your ideas are worth trying. Organize your ideas so that they are clear to the reader. Use correct grammar, punctuation, and spelling.

For the past weeks recess has been every kids nightmare. Unpleasant arguments, fights it's total kaos. Kids are even scared to go out to recess.

If our school wants to be peaceful again we have to have everyone help. First we have to have some rules. We should have consequences. If students behave and help enforce rules they should be rewarded. Those who disobey should be penalized.

If we want a great school we all have to work together.

Prompt for a Writing Sample — Grade 6

Student Writing Sample

(2+)

Name *Don Murray*   Date *11-25-92*

Writing Situation

The students in your school have been having trouble getting along at recess and lunchtime. There have been unpleasant arguments and even one fight. Many of the students are very upset about this situation. Some of them are afraid to go out on the field to join in the games.

Directions for Writing

Think of an idea or two for helping to solve this problem and write an article for your school newspaper describing your plan. Try to write in such a way that you will convince your readers (both students and teachers) that your ideas are worth trying. Organize your ideas so that they are clear to the reader. Use correct grammar, punctuation, and spelling.

> There is a big problem in our school. The students are having trouble getting along at recess. One way to solve this problem is to get yard duties out watching the games. Another reason is to make a very bad punishment for someone who gets into a fight. Finally I would call the parents. I the same person gets caught a second time they will stay after school for a half hour. If they get caught again they will stay after school for an hour. If there is ever a fourth time you get suspended.

Prompt for a Writing Sample — Grade 6

Student Writing Sample

(1+)

Name _Rob Phillips_　　　　　Date _Nov. 24, 1992_

Writing Situation

The students in your school have been having trouble getting along at recess and lunchtime. There have been unpleasant arguments and even one fight. Many of the students are very upset about this situation. Some of them are afraid to go out on the field to join in the games.

Directions for Writing

Think of an idea or two for helping to solve this problem and write an article for your school newspaper describing your plan. Try to write in such a way that you will convince your readers (both students and teachers) that your ideas are worth trying. Organize your ideas so that they are clear to the reader. Use correct grammar, punctuation, and spelling.

> Dear Parents and Students
> "We have a problem a our school"
> stated Mrs. Smith. Comeing from me.
> "I think there is to many fights
> just yesterday Billy and Joe were fighting
> because of team leader?" "Football is
> our main problem, because it should not
> be tackle." "I think that kids shuid have
> fun at lunch time." "Kids that get in a
> fight shuid be in a lot of troble." "I think
> we can make a difference in our school."
> We want more yard dudtys on the black
> top." "Thanks you for your tine."
> 　　　Student of Clinton
> 　　　　Rob Phillips

Do-It-Yourself Directions:
A Personal Rubric Workshop

Why Do I Want to Write a Rubric?

There are a number of reasons for wanting to write a rubric of your own:

1. You know what you have been teaching.

2. You know what you expect your students to have mastered.

3. You know what separates excellent and average achievement from achievement that needs remediation.

4. Ready-made rubrics do not reflect your curriculum or your expectations.

How Do I Begin?

First of all, it is important to know that your prompt and your rubric are part of the same package.

Secondly, it is vital to realize that this is an interactive procedure — you will write, try out, and revise your prompt/rubric package until it tells you what you really want to know. Getting it exactly right the first time is a result of years of experience or plain luck!

Write the Rubric First

It is probably easier to write the rubric first. If you review the level at which your students are working and isolate the skills you want them to have, you are well on your way. A three-point rubric is the easiest, and you can begin at any point.

The three points of a three-point rubric parallel one another and reflect different levels of the same skills. The "High Pass" contains all of the features of the "Pass" either in identical form or as a more advanced variation. "Needs Revision" considers parallel features but they may be expressed as negatives. If you look back at the grade 1 scoring rubric on page 17, you can see this very clearly demonstrated. Both the "High Pass" and the "Pass" require the student to respond to the prompt. "Needs Revision" states that the student "may not respond to the prompt."

The other points are also variations on the levels of achievement in specific skills. The person who wrote this rubric (SCORING RUBRIC — GRADE 1) was evidently teaching and assessing the ability of students to write sentences. He or she was also looking at the process of invented or approximated spelling. This same parallel development can be traced in the sample rubrics at all of the grade levels.

Do-It-Yourself Directions:
A Personal Rubric Workshop *(cont.)*

If you are looking at another skill, you would decide on what, for you, would be acceptable performance, and that would be your "Pass." You would decide what level of expertise would exceed the ''average'' expectations and make that your "High Pass." Then you would decide on the characteristic of a sample that would keep it from passing and write that variation in the section we are calling "Needs Revision." Once you have decided on a skill to include in your rubric, it must appear in some form in all of the points.

Write the Prompt

Your prompt should be written to elicit a response that will allow assessment of the points in your rubric. If your "High Pass" requires the students to write more than one complete sentence, you should not instruct them to write "a sentence." This seems really obvious, but sometimes you will not catch this kind of thing until you are reading a batch of papers. If you suddenly realize that you are not getting any high papers, you may want to look back at the wording of your prompt.

Revise, Revise, Revise

There are many reasons to consider revising your rubric and/or prompt. Look for some of these:

1. No high papers

   — Did I require something I have not taught?

   — Did I require something in the rubric I did not ask for in the prompt?

2. All high papers

   — Did I place my expectations too low?

   — Did I want this result? (It is possible for everyone to do really well.)

3. No passing papers

   — Were the directions wrong or easy to misinterpret?

   — Was the format different from our usual assignments?

4. Results inconsistent with the way I see my class

   — Do I need to look at the prompt/rubric package?

   — Do I need to take another look at the class?

Rubrics Are Power

Feeling comfortable with rubric-writing gives you a power position in the assessment process. You will always be able to justify your results and demonstrate how you obtained them.

Do-It-Yourself Teacher Script

Use this blank form to create your own teacher script for a writing sample prompt.

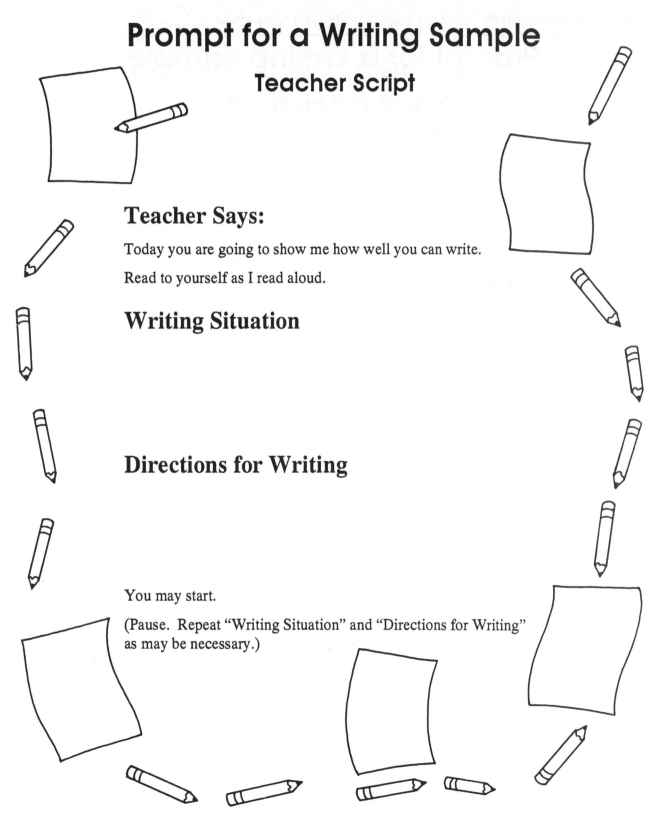

Prompt for a Writing Sample
Teacher Script

Teacher Says:

Today you are going to show me how well you can write.

Read to yourself as I read aloud.

Writing Situation

Directions for Writing

You may start.

(Pause. Repeat "Writing Situation" and "Directions for Writing" as may be necessary.)

Do-It-Yourself
Student Writing Sample

Use this blank form to create your own Student Writing Sample prompt.

- -

Prompt for a Writing Sample

Student Writing Sample

Name _____   Date _____

Writing Situation

Directions for Writing

_____

_____

_____

_____

_____

_____

_____

_____

_____

_____

_____

_____

_____

_____

Do-It-Yourself Rubric

Use this blank form to create your own scoring rubric for a writing sample.

Scoring Rubric

Score 3: *High Pass*

Student

-
-
-

Score 2: *Pass*

Student

-
-
-

Score 1: *Needs Revision*

Student

-
-
-

Score 0: *No Response*

Generalized Task Rubric

The generalized task rubric below is a more complex version of the DO-IT-YOURSELF RUBRIC on the preceding page. It can be used as a "template" from which to build specific elaborated rubrics.

An elaborated rubric (see pages 59, 65, and 71) can be devised to fit a particular prompt in any subject area by adding specific elements to the categories in the generalized rubric, building both up and down the scale from Score 4 which is the midpoint.

Scores 6 and 5 would be considered high papers, Scores 4 and 3 would be high/low average, and Scores 2 and 1 would be attempts that "need revision" or "need correction." Failure is not part of teaching with a rubric, since the student can always try again.

On the next pages you will find examples of prompts for open ended math problems. These include teacher scripts, forms for the student samples, and rubrics that have been elaborated with details appropriate to each prompt. A range of student work follows each set of forms.

Generalized Task Rubric

Score 6: *Exemplary Achievement*

Score 5: *Commendable Achievement*

Score 4: *Adequate Achievement*

(Demonstrates a general understanding of the major concepts.)

Score 3: *Some Evidence Of Achievement*

Score 2: *Limited Evidence Of Achievement*

Score 1: *Minimal Evidence Of Achievement*

Score 0: *No Response*

Prompt for a Math Problem — Grade 1 or 2

Teacher Script

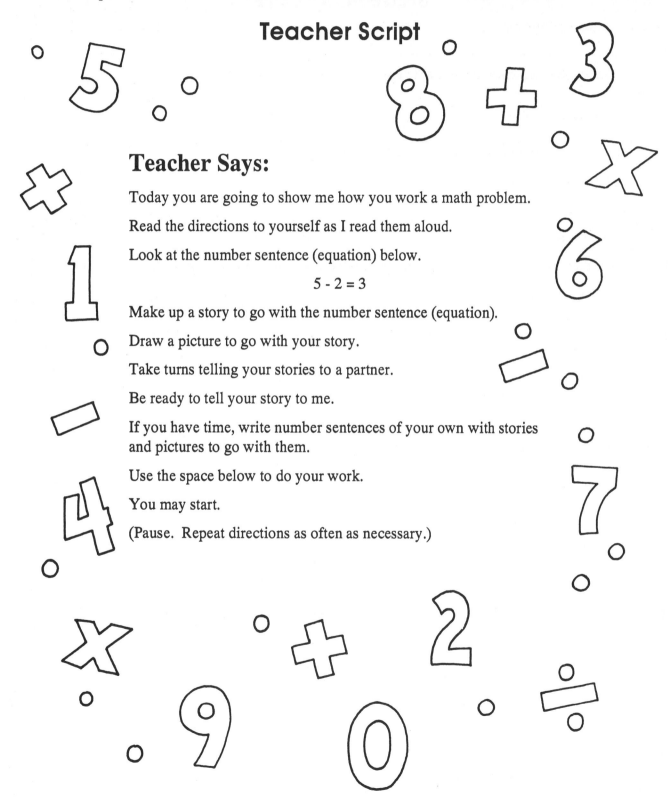

Teacher Says:

Today you are going to show me how you work a math problem.

Read the directions to yourself as I read them aloud.

Look at the number sentence (equation) below.

$$5 - 2 = 3$$

Make up a story to go with the number sentence (equation).

Draw a picture to go with your story.

Take turns telling your stories to a partner.

Be ready to tell your story to me.

If you have time, write number sentences of your own with stories and pictures to go with them.

Use the space below to do your work.

You may start.

(Pause. Repeat directions as often as necessary.)

Prompt for a Math Problem — Grade 1 or 2

Student Sample

Name _____   Date _____

Look at the number sentence (equation) below.

$$5 - 2 = 3$$

Make up a story to go with the number sentence (equation).

Draw a picture to go with your story.

Take turns telling your stories to a partner.

Be ready to tell your story to me.

If you have time, write number sentences of your own with stories and pictures to go with them.

Use the space below to do your work.

Use this RUBRIC with the TEACHER SCRIPT (page 57) and STUDENT SAMPLE form (page 58) to generate a math assessment to include in your students' portfolios.

Elaborated Task Rubric for a Math Problem — Grade 1 or 2

Score 6: *Exemplary Achievement*

- Demonstrates internalized understanding of major concepts
  - Draws a picture that clearly illustrates given equation in both number and operation
  - Creates an appropriate story to go with illustration for equation as evidenced by oral telling of story
  - Creates additional equations, stories, illustrations

Score 5: *Commendable Achievement*

- Demonstrates detailed understanding of major concepts
  - Draws a pictures that clearly illustrates given equation in both number and operation
  - Creates an appropriate story to go with illustration for equation as evidenced by oral telling of story

Score 4: *Adequate Achievement*

- Demonstrates a general understanding of the major concepts
  - Either creates an appropriate story to go with equation as evidenced by oral telling of story or draws a picture that clearly illustrates equation

Score 3: *Some Evidence of Achievement*

- Demonstrates a partial understanding of the major concepts
  - Creates a story or draws a picture that reflects either the total number of objects required by the equation or the operation involved

Score 2: *Limited Evidence of Achievement*

- Demonstrates a lack of skills necessary to reach solution
  - Draws a picture or tells a story that has little or nothing to do with the given equation

Score 1: *Minimal Evidence of Achievement*

- Demonstrates a lack of understanding
  - Misinterprets problem or directions or both

Score 0: *No Response*

This STUDENT SAMPLE is an example of a response to the prompt and rubric set on the preceding pages.

Prompt for a Math Problem — Grade 1 or 2

Student Sample

Name _Helena_   Date _Feb. 4, 1993_

Look at the number sentence (equation) below.

$$5 - 2 = 3$$

Make up a story to go with the number sentence (equation).

Draw a picture to go with your story.

Take turns telling your stories to a partner.

Be ready to tell your story to me.

If you have time, write number sentences of your own with stories and pictures to go with them.

Use the space below to do your work.

This STUDENT SAMPLE is an example of a response to the prompt and rubric set on the preceding pages.

Prompt for a Math Problem — Grade 1 or 2

Student Sample

Name **Melanie**   Date **feb. 4, 1993**

Look at the number sentence (equation) below.

$$5 - 2 = 3$$

Make up a story to go with the number sentence (equation).

Draw a picture to go with your story.

Take turns telling your stories to a partner.

Be ready to tell your story to me.

If you have time, write number sentences of your own with stories and pictures to go with them.

Use the space to do your work.

This STUDENT SAMPLE is an example of a response to the prompt and rubric set on the preceding pages.

Prompt for a Math Problem — Grade 1 or 2

Student Sample

Name **Tran**   Date **Feb. 4, 1993.**

Look at the number sentence (equation) below.

5 - 2 = 3

2

Make up a story to go with the number sentence (equation).

Draw a picture to go with your story.

Take turns telling your stories to a partner.

Be ready to tell your story to me.

If you have time, write number sentences of your own with stories and pictures to go with them.

Use the space below to do your work.

Prompt for a Math Problem — Grade 3 or 4

Teacher Script

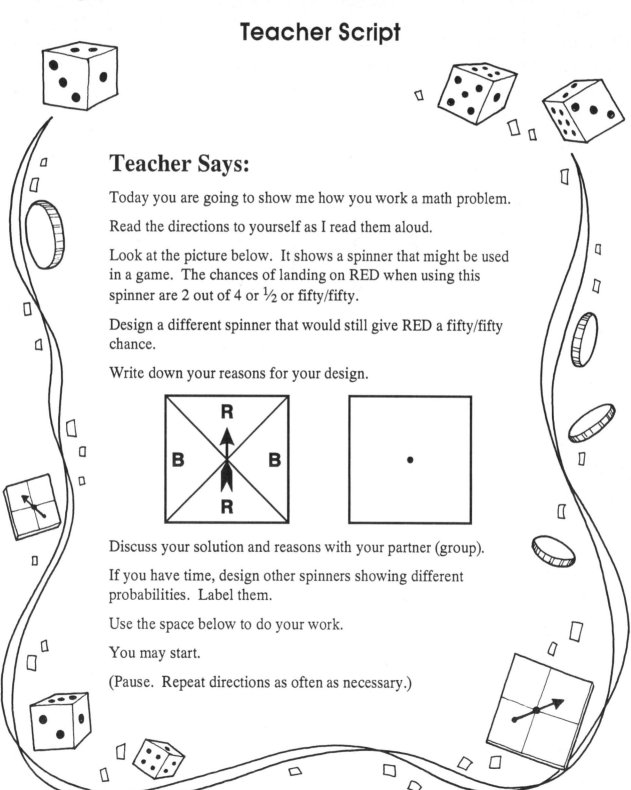

Teacher Says:

Today you are going to show me how you work a math problem.

Read the directions to yourself as I read them aloud.

Look at the picture below. It shows a spinner that might be used in a game. The chances of landing on RED when using this spinner are 2 out of 4 or $\frac{1}{2}$ or fifty/fifty.

Design a different spinner that would still give RED a fifty/fifty chance.

Write down your reasons for your design.

Discuss your solution and reasons with your partner (group).

If you have time, design other spinners showing different probabilities. Label them.

Use the space below to do your work.

You may start.

(Pause. Repeat directions as often as necessary.)

Use this STUDENT SAMPLE form together with the TEACHER SCRIPT (page 63) and the RUBRIC (page 65) to generate a math assessment to include in your students' portfolios.

Prompt for a Math Problem — Grade 3 or 4

Student Sample

Name _____ Date _____

Look at the picture below. It shows a spinner that might be used in a game. The chances of landing on RED when using this spinner are 2 out of 4 or ½ or fifty/fifty.

Design a different spinner that would still give RED a fifty/fifty chance.

Write down your reasons for your design.

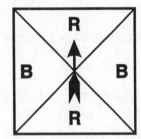 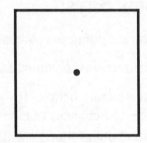

Discuss your solution and reasons with your partner (group).

If you have time, design other spinners showing different probabilities. Label them.

Use the space below to do your work.

Use this RUBRIC with the TEACHER SCRIPT (page 63) and STUDENT SAMPLE form (page 64) it to generate a math assessment to include in your students' portfolios.

Elaborated Task Rubric for a Math Problem — Grade 3 or 4

Score 6: *Exemplary Achievement*

- Demonstrates internalized understanding of major concepts
  - — Draws a spinner that clearly illustrates another way to show a fifty/fifty chance for RED
  - — Writes a clear and accurate reason for his/her design and is able to discuss with partner (group)
  - — Creates additional spinners and labels them correctly

Score 5: *Commendable Achievement*

- Demonstrates detailed understanding of major concepts
  - — Draws a spinner that clearly illustrates another way to show a fifty/fifty chance for RED
  - — Writes a clear and accurate reason for his/her design and is able to discuss with partner (group)

Score 4: *Adequate Achievement*

- Demonstrates a general understanding of the major concepts
  - — Draws a spinner that clearly illustrates another way to show a fifty/fifty chance for RED
  - — Attempts to write or explain design orally but is only partially successful

Score 3: *Some Evidence of Achievement*

- Demonstrates a partial understanding of the major concepts
  - — Draws correct spinner but makes no attempt to explain reasoning

Score 2: *Limited Evidence of Achievement*

- Demonstrates a lack of skills necessary to reach solution
  - — Draws spinner or gives reasons that have little to do with the original problem

Score 1: *Minimal Evidence of Achievement*

- Demonstrates a lack of understanding
  - — Misinterprets problem or directions or both

Score 0: *No Response*

Prompt for a Math Problem — Grade 3 or 4

Student Sample

Name __Mark M.__   Date __2-10-93__

Look at the picture below. It shows a spinner that might be used in a game. The chances of landing on RED when using this spinner are 2 out of 4 or ½ or fifty/fifty.

④

Design a different spinner that would still give RED a fifty/fifty chance.

Write down your reasons for your design.

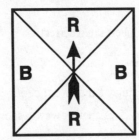 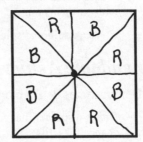

Discuss your solution and reasons with your partner (group).

If you have time, design other spinners showing different probabilities. Label them.

Use the space below to do your work.

Red has an equal chance because there is
four red triangles and four triangles of
blue. So four and four are equal.

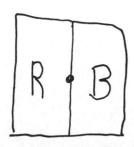

This STUDENT SAMPLE is an example of a response to the prompt and rubric set on the preceding pages.

Prompt for a Math Problem — Grade 3 or 4

Student Sample

Name _Megan_   Date _Feb. 10, 93_

Look at the picture below. It shows a spinner that might be used in a game. The chances of landing on RED when using this spinner are 2 out of 4 or ½ or fifty/fifty.

Design a different spinner that would still give RED a fifty/fifty chance.

Write down your reasons for your design.

$$\boxed{3}$$

Discuss your solution and reasons with your partner (group).

If you have time, design other spinners showing different probabilities. Label them.

Use the space below to do your work.

2 out of 2 chances it
will be Red

Prompt for a Math Problem — Grade 3 or 4

Student Sample

Name _Marty_ Date _____

Look at the picture below. It shows a spinner that might be used in a game. The chances of landing on RED when using this spinner are 2 out of 4 or ½ or fifty/fifty.

Design a different spinner that would still give RED a fifty/fifty chance.

Write down your reasons for your design.

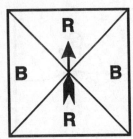 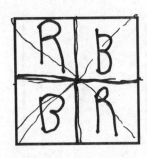 

Discuss your solution and reasons with your partner (group).

If you have time, design other spinners showing different probabilities. Label them.

Use the space below to do your work.

So you can spin at any speed and you might just hit red.

 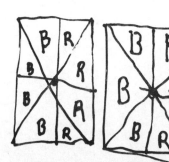

Use this TEACHER SCRIPT together with the STUDENT SAMPLE form (page 70) and RUBRIC (page 71) to generate a math assessment to include in your students' portfolios.

Prompt for a Math Problem — Grade 5 or 6

Teacher Script

Teacher Says:

Today you are going to show me how you work a math problem.

Read the directions to yourself as I read them aloud.

Solve the following problem. Describe your method and show your work. Draw a diagram that shows how you thought about the problem. Include "false starts" as well as successful methods. Explain why you rejected the methods you decided not to use. Reflect on your solution. Try to make a generalization about it.

A student has three pairs of pants — black, brown, and white — as well as three shirts in the same colors. How many different outfits can be made by combining these pants and shirts in different ways?

If you have time, create another problem of this kind. Ask your partner to solve it.

Use the space below to do your work.

You may start.

(Pause. Repeat directions as often as necessary.)

Prompt for a Math Problem — Grade 5 or 6

Student Sample

Name _____   Date _____

Solve the following problem. Describe your method and show your work. Draw a diagram that shows how you thought about the problem. Include "false starts" as well as successful methods. Explain why you rejected the methods you decided not to use. Reflect on your solution. Try to make a generalization about it.

A student has three pairs of pants — black, brown, and white — as well as three shirts in the same colors. How many different outfits can be made by combining these pants and shirts in different ways?

If you have time, create another problem of this kind. Ask your partner to solve it.

Use the space below to do your work.

70

Use this RUBRIC with the TEACHER SCRIPT and STUDENT SAMPLE form that precede it to generate a math assessment to include in your students' portfolios.

Elaborated Task for a
Math Problem — Grade 5 or 6

Score 6: *Exemplary Achievement*

- Demonstrates internalized understanding of major concepts
  - Solves Problem and gets correct answer
  - Shows computation, draws and labels diagram
  - Includes alternative attempts to think about problem
  - Reflects on and generalizes about methods and solutions

Score 5: *Commendable Achievement*

- Demonstrates detailed understanding of major concepts
  - Solves problem and gets correct answer
  - Shows computation, draws and labels diagram
  - Includes alternative attempts to think about problem

Score 4: *Adequate Achievement*

- Demonstrates a general understanding of the major concepts
  - Solves problem and gets correct answer
  - Shows computation and gets correct answer

Score 3: *Some Evidence of Achievement*

- Demonstrates a partial understanding of the major concepts
  - Solves problem
  - Computation and/or diagram not consistent with solution

Score 2: *Limited Evidence of Achievement*

- Demonstrates a lack of skills necessary to reach solution
  - Draws incorrect diagram or makes incorrect computation

Score 1: *Minimal Evidence of Achievement*

- Demonstrates a lack of understanding
  - Misinterprets problem or directions or both

Score 0: *No Response*

This STUDENT SAMPLE is an example of a response to the prompt and rubric set on the preceding pages.

Prompt for a Math Problem — Grade 5 or 6

Student Sample

(5)

Name _Trixie Mandyn_   Date _February 10, 1993_

Solve the following problem. Describe your method and show your work. Draw a diagram that shows how you thought about the problem. Include "false starts" as well as successful methods. Explain why you rejected the methods you decided not to use. Reflect on your solution. Try to make a generalization about it.

A student has three pairs of pants — black, brown, and white — as well as three shirts in the same colors. How many different outfits can be made by combining these pants and shirts in different ways?

If you have time, create another problem of this kind. Ask your partner to solve it. _9 different ways_

Use the space below to do your work.

Pants	Shirts	Pants	Shirts
B	B	B ⟋⟍ B	
Br	Br	Br ⤬ Br	
Bl	Bl	Bl ⟍⟋ Bl	

B = black

Br = brown

Bl = black

This STUDENT SAMPLE is an example of a response to the prompt and rubric set on the preceding pages.

Prompt for a Math Problem — Grade 5 or 6

Student Sample

(4-)

Name _D. J. Lewis_   Date _2/10/93_

Solve the following problem. Describe your method and show your work. Draw a diagram that shows how you thought about the problem. Include "false starts" as well as successful methods. Explain why you rejected the methods you decided not to use. Reflect on your solution. Try to make a generalization about it.

A student has three pairs of pants — black, brown, and white — as well as three shirts in the same colors. How many different outfits can be made by combining these pants and shirts in different ways?

If you have time, create another problem of this kind. Ask your partner to solve it.

Use the space below to do your work.

Bl — Bl   W — Br

Br — Br   Br — Bl

W — W   Bl — ~~~~ W

3

W — Bl

Bl — Br

Br — ~~~~ W

This STUDENT SAMPLE is an example of a response to the prompt and rubric set on the preceding pages.

Prompt for a Math Problem — Grade 5 or 6

Student Sample

(2)

Name _MONICA PEREZ_   Date _FEB. 10_

Solve the following problem. Describe your method and show your work. Draw a diagram that shows how you thought about the problem. Include "false starts" as well as successful methods. Explain why you rejected the methods you decided not to use. Reflect on your solution. Try to make a generalization about it.

A student has three pairs of pants — black, brown, and white — as well as three shirts in the same colors. How many different outfits can be made by combining these pants and shirts in different ways?

If you have time, create another problem of this kind. Ask your partner to solve it.

Use the space below to do your work.

BLACK - PANTS - WHITE SHIRT, BROWN SHIRT
BROWN - PANTS - WHITE SHIRT, BLACK SHIRT
WHITE - PANTS - BLACK SHIRT, BROWN SHIRT

This is an example of how to use this form to keep track of your individual students and their progress in writing throughout the year. A good time to do this is when they look over their work in order to reflect on their own progress.

Individual Student Summary
of Progress in Writing

✓ ___ Means Mastery

Name Tran Nguyen   **Date** 2-7-93

Prompts	1	2	3	4	5	6	7	8
Over-All Score (3, 2, 1, 0)	③	②						
Mastery/Genre	pers. exp.	auto-bio						
Organization	✓	✓						
Mechanics/Sentences	✓	run-ons						
Mechanics/Usage	verb agree	✓						
Mechanics/Punctuation	?	✓						
Mechanics/Capitals	✓	✓						
Mechanics/Spelling	phonetic	phonetic						
District Objectives								
LA 1.2.2 end punctuation		✓						
LA 2.2.3 caps.	✓	✓						
LA 3.3.1 spelling	phonetic							

Run off copies of this form to keep track of your individual students and their progress in writing throughout the year. A good time to do this is when they look over their work in order to reflect on their own progress.

Individual Student Summary of Progress in Writing

_____ Means Mastery

Name					Date			

Prompts	1	2	3	4	5	6	7	8
Over-All Score (3, 2, 1, 0)								
Mastery/Genre								
Organization								
Mechanics/Sentences								
Mechanics/Usage								
Mechanics/Punctuation								
Mechanics/Capitals								
Mechanics/Spelling								
District Objectives								

This is an example of how to use this form to keep track of your individual students and their progress in math throughout the year. A good time to do this is when they look over their work in order to reflect on their own progress.

Individual Student Summary of Progress in Math

___✓___ **Means Mastery**

Name *Laura Gonzalez* ✓   Date   9-7-93

Prompts	1	2	3	4	5	6	7	8
Over-All Score (6, 5, 4, 3, 2, 1, 0)	④	⑤						
Math	numbers	patterns						
Understands Concept(s)	✓	✓						
Records Attempts	✓	✓						
Formulates Equation(s)		✓						
Draws Pictures/Diagrams	✓	✓						
Gets "Answer"	✓							
Extends Experience		✓						
District Objectives								
MA 1.1.1 *simple addition*	✓							
MA 1.2.1 *knows operation*		✓						
MA 2.3.1 *extends pattern*		✓						

Run off copies of this form to keep track of your individual students and their progress in math throughout the year. A good time to do this is when they look over their work in order to reflect on their own progress.

Individual Student Summary of Progress in Math

_____ Means Mastery

Name					Date			

Prompts	1	2	3	4	5	6	7	8
Over-All Score (6, 5, 4, 3, 2, 1, 0)								
Math								
Understands Concept(s)								
Records Attempts								
Formulates Equation(s)								
Draws Pictures/Diagrams								
Gets "Answer"								
Extends Experience								
District Objectives								

This is an example of how to use this form to keep track of your whole class and get an at-a-glance overview of who needs to do what. Here rubric scores have been used. A simple check mark for mastery would also be effective.

Whole Class
Summary of Progress in ___Writing___

Name	Prompt # and Score							
Aden, June	¹/③	²/②	³/③	⁴/__	⁵/__	⁶/②		
Blanco, Marcos	¹/①	²/①	³/①	⁴/②	⁵/②	⁶/①		
Cooper, Brianna	¹/③	²/__	³/③	⁴/③	⁵/__	⁶/__		

Run off copies of this form and use them to keep track of your whole class and get an at-a-glance overview of who needs to do what.

Whole Class
Summary of Progress in _____

Name	Prompt # and Score						

Assigned-Task Assessment: What, How, When, and Why

The 3 P's

The "3 R's" of Alternative Assessment — Rubrics, 'Riting, and 'Rithmetic — have already been introduced in the preceding pages. Now let's take a look at the 3 P's. The 3 P's of alternative assessment are Portfolios, Performances, and Projects.

Portfolios

Portfolios form a general and multi-dimensional background for alternative assessment methods. More ways to use them will be discussed in the last section of this book.

Performances and Projects

Performances and projects are a good example of assessment that is trying to be authentic. The assigned tasks that prompt these two kinds of assessment should come as close as possible to "real life" activities. They should possess the characteristics that identify them as alternative assessments: They should be complex (involving a group of learning behaviors), open-ended (permitting more than one solution), and coherent (resulting in a single product).

Performances

As is true with the term "portfolio," performance assessment is a general, multiple-meaning term too. It covers writing assessments and some open-ended math assessments in which the end product of the student's performance is rated or scored. In these examples, the assessment is considered performance assessment because the student has generated the product which can then be scored with a rubric. Performance assessment can also be the actual observation of the student-in-action. This process of observation might consist of watching a student do a science experiment or participate in a cooperative learning group. This kind of performance assessment can be documented with a checklist.

Projects

Projects qualify as a kind of performance assessment in two ways: They are generated by the student and they take long enough to allow for observing the student-in-action. They can be documented in many ways. The observer can use a checklist. The activities can be photographed and/or filmed with a video camera. Any oral component can be taped. The project can include a written component. All of the pieces — the evidence, so to speak — can be collected and stored in a portfolio. Projects are often associated with the social studies curriculum.

Chris Barron's Project

Assigned-Task Assessment:
What, How, When, And Why *(cont.)*

So What Are Checklists?

Checklists are important because they go with many kinds of alternative assessments. They document performances and projects. They fit right into portfolios. At first mention, checklists sound easy and self-explanatory. They are, of course, lists of things to be checked off by the observer in the course of observing a performance. But what things? That is the important and very controversial question.

We have gotten into the habit of depending on objective, multiple-choice tests designed to measure incremental and usually minimum proficiency skills to tell us what our students know. For instance, many reading tests measure knowledge of phonics. A good reader — someone who can read words and comprehend their meaning — who learned to read by generalizing from a sight vocabulary might easily fail a phonics tests.

And How Do We Make a Checklist?

So how do we make our checklist? We do what is called a task analysis. We figure out what really goes into the achievement of a particular end. In the case of a reading test, we would have to define what we meant by reading. Hard as that might be, it is easy compared to deciding what we mean by knowing or understanding or using science, for example.

We will have to remember that performance is knowledge in use. We must look for evidence that knowledge has been acquired and then look at the competence and originality with which that knowledge is applied to the given problem. We must leave out things that do not really support the evidence we are looking for and put in the things that are important. This process is going to take some time. Many assessment experts are concerned that we will make ourselves and our system accountable before we have time to try it out, see what does and does not work, and become comfortable with it.

Another approach to the checklist is to simply take a curriculum scope-and-sequence chart or a district framework and use it. You will need to add some criteria to tell you how you will recognize that the content is there and how well it has been achieved. If your science curriculum says something like this, you can turn it into a checklist and just use it:

1.0 Understands/uses scientific method

1.1 Identifies problem

1.2 Poses hypothesis

1.3 Creates experiment

1.4 Gathers/records evidence

1.5 Makes generalization

See the following pages for examples of how to document a performance assessment and forms to use in your own classroom.

Task Analyses, Observations and Checklists in Action

Sectional Table of Contents

Use these questions to help you decide on a task to prompt your performance assessment. Add more if you wish.

- -

Selecting a Task —
Questions to Ask Yourself

Task Being Considered

_____

_____

_____

_____

Questions to Ask

1. Does this task match my instructional goals? Which ones?

_____

_____

_____

2. Will the completed task reflect the skills and knowledge I want my students to acquire? What are they?

_____

_____

_____

3. Are several disciplines represented in the task? Which ones?

_____

_____

_____

4. Will the task measure more than one goal? If so, what are they?

_____

_____

_____

Use these questions to help you describe the task you choose. Add other questions that are relevant or important to you.

Describing the Task
Questions to Ask Yourself

Task Being Considered

_____

_____

_____

_____

Questions to Ask

1. How will the questions to the students be asked? Give examples.

    _____

    _____

    _____

    _____

2. Will the work be done as individuals or as groups? Describe.

    _____

    _____

    _____

    _____

3. What materials will I need? List.

    _____

    _____

    _____

    _____

4. How much time will be allowed? Will all of the work be done at school or will homework be assigned?

    _____

    _____

    _____

    _____

Use these questions to help you decide on scoring criteria. Add others that are important to you.

Setting Scoring Criteria — Questions to Ask Yourself

Task Being Considered

_____

_____

_____

_____

Questions to Ask

1. How will I know that students have made an excellent response? An acceptable response? A poor response?

_____

_____

_____

_____

2. Do I have models of responses that reflect various skill levels?

_____

_____

_____

_____

3. How does completion of this task relate to my instructional goals?

_____

_____

_____

_____

4. How does completion of this task relate to district/state goals?

_____

_____

_____

_____

This is an example of how to use a checklist to document your observation of literal comprehension in first or second grade readers.

Individual Checklist for
Literal Comprehension in Reading
Grade 1 or 2

Name _Marissa_   Date _12/5/92_

Title of Story _Three Billy Goats Gruff_

Behavior	Observed			
	Poor to Excellent			
	1	2	3	4
Can answer questions about details from the story (literal details). *Where did the troll live?*				✓
Can retell story, including all main events (main idea). *Tell me the story in your words.*			✓	
Can retell story in chronological order (sequence). *Tell me the story in order— beginning to end.*			✓	
Can answer questions about *first*, *last*, etc. (sequence). *Which Billy Goat crossed the bridge first?*		✓		
Defines words from the story (vocabulary). *What does "huff" mean?*		✓		
Recognizes and explains effects of affix on a word in the story (vocabulary). *The "re" in "return" makes the word mean...*	✓			

Use this checklist to document your observation of literal comprehension in first or second grade readers.

Individual Checklist for
Literal Comprehension in Reading
Grade 1 or 2

Name _____   Date _____

Title of Story _____

Behavior	Observed			
	Poor to Excellent			
	1	2	3	4
Can answer questions about details from the story (literal details).				
Can retell story, including all main events (main idea).				
Can retell story in chronological order (sequence).				
Can answer questions about *first, last,* etc. (sequence).				
Defines words from the story (vocabulary).				
Recognizes and explains effects of affix on a word in the story (vocabulary).				

This is an example of how to use a classroom checklist to compile results from individual checklists.

Classroom Checklist • Literal Comprehension
Grade 1 or 2

"Three Billy Goats Gruff"	Literal details	Main idea	Sequence #1	Sequence #2	Sight vocab.	Affixes	Comments
Adams, Clark	✓	✓					small group- sequence
Alvarez, Laura	✓	✓	✓				"
O'Reilly, Brenda	✓	✓	✓	✓	✓	✓	Wow!
Wellman, Brent			✓	✓			review detail + M.I.

Use this classroom checklist to compile results from individual checklists. Run off enough copies to accommodate all students in your class.

Classroom Checklist • Literal Comprehension
Grade 1 or 2

This is an example of how to use a checklist to document your observation of inferential comprehension in third or fourth grade readers.

Checklist for Inferential Comprehension in Reading
Grade 3 or 4

Name **Danny Janson**   Date **2/15/93**

Title of Story **Stone Fox by John Gardiner**

Behavior	Observed			
	Poor to Excellent			
	1	2	3	4
Can express the unstated main idea of a story. Tell me what the story was about in your own words.			✓	
Can answer questions relating to cause/effect relationships. Why does Little Willy enter the race?				✓
Can predict outcomes. What do you think will happen to Little Willy after the race?				✓
Can compare and contrast. How are Little Willy's and Stone Fox's reasons for wanting the money alike?		✓		
Can draw conclusions. Why did Stone Fox do what he did?			✓	

Use this checklist to document your observations of inferential comprehension in third or fourth grade readers.

Checklist for Inferential Comprehension in Reading
Grade 3 or 4

Name _____   Date _____

Title of Story _____

Behavior	Observed			
	Poor to Excellent			
	1	2	3	4
Can express the unstated main idea of a story.				
Can answer questions relating to cause/effect relationships.				
Can predict outcomes.				
Can compare and contrast.				
Can draw conclusions.				

This is an example of how to use a classroom checklist to compile results from individual checklists.

Classroom Checklist ▪ Inferential Comprehension
Grade 3 or 4

Stone Fox	Unstated Main Idea	Cause/Effect	Predict	Compare/ Contrast	Draw Conclusions		Comments
Dunbar, Inez	✓	✓	✓		✓		Doesn't get comparison
Janson, Danny	✓	✓	✓	✓	✓	✓	No problem
Lee, Cliff	✓		✓	✓	✓		Mixes cause/ effect with seq.
Pham, Thuy Thanh							ESL

Use this classroom checklist to compile results from individual checklists. Run off enough copies to accommodate all the students in your class.

Classroom Checklist ▪ Inferential Comprehension
Grade 3 or 4

This is an example of how to use a checklist to document your observation of interpretive comprehension in fifth or sixth grade readers.

- -

Checklist for Interpretive Comprehension in Reading

Grade 5 or 6

Name _Tabitha Buckley_   Date _1-30-93_

Title of Story _The Friendship by Mildred D. Taylor_

Behavior	Observed			
	Poor to Excellent			
	1	2	3	4
Analyzes character. Why does John Wallace break his promise to Tom?		✓		
Understands setting. Describe the time and place of this story.				✓
Summarizes plot. How did the can of sardines move the plot along?			✓	
Understands dialogue. Find a quote that shows how Tom feels.			✓	
Senses mood. What word best expresses the mood of the story?			✓	
Understands genre. What type of literature is The Friendship?		✓		

Use this checklist to document your observation of interpretive comprehension in fifth or sixth grade readers.

Checklist for Interpretive Comprehension in Reading

Grade 5 or 6

Name _____   Date _____

Title of Story _____

Behavior	Observed			
	Poor to Excellent			
	1	2	3	4
Analyzes character.				
Understands setting.				
Summarizes plot.				
Understands dialogue.				
Senses mood.				
Understands genre.				

This is an example of how to use a classroom checklist to compile results from individual checklists.

Classroom Checklist • Interpretive Comprehension
Grade 5 or 6

The Friendship	Character	Setting	Plot	Dialogue	Mood	Genre	Comments
Buckley, Sabitha	✓	✓	✓	✓	✓	✓	Good!
Hoskins, Tracy							needs vocab. to discuss
Marquez, Roberto	✓	✓	✓	✓			
Montague, Juliet	✓				✓		work with aide

Use this classroom checklist to compile results from individual checklists. Run off enough copies to accommodate all the students in your class.

Classroom Checklist • Interpretive Comprehension
Grade 5 or 6

This is an example of how to use a checklist to document your observation of a science task for first or second graders.

Checklist for Science — Grade 1 or 2

Name _Lisa Pham_   Date _3/4/93_

Task: Student will apply the scientific method by recording his/her observations during an assigned science task. The task will consist of examining a lima bean that has been soaked in water to identify the little plant (embryo) inside. The student will then draw and write about what he/she saw.

Behavior	Observed Poor to Excellent			
	1	2	3	4
Follows directions (breaks open seed, uses magnifying glass, etc.). _Responded to both oral and written directions_				✓
Compares real plant embryo with book or other illustrations.				✓
Discusses findings with cooperative-learning partner or group. _Assumed leadership of groups_				✓
Draws what he/she observed on outline of bean seed.				✓
Makes science journal entry describing experience. _Excellent comprehension of concepts evidenced_				✓

Use this checklist to document your observation of a science task for first or second graders.

Checklist for Science — Grade 1 or 2

Name _____   Date _____

Task: _____

_____

_____

Behavior	Observed Poor to Excellent			
	1	2	3	4
Follows directions.				
Compares _____ with book or other illustrations.				
Discusses findings with cooperative-learning partner or group.				
Draws what he/she observed.				
Makes science journal entry describing experience.				

This is an example of how to use a classroom checklist to compile results from individual checklists.

Classroom Checklist for Task Observation in Science
Grade 1 or 2

Bean Seed Observation	Follows directions	Compares	Discusses	Draws diagram	Writes journal entry		Comments
Hollis, Fred	✓	✓		✓	✓		needs more group work
Mitrevski, Nancy				✓			ESL
Pham, Lisa	✓	✓	✓	✓	✓		a scientist!

Use this classroom checklist to compile results from individual checklists. Run off enough copies to accommodate all the students in your class.

Classroom Checklist for Task Observation in Science
Grade 1 or 2

This is an example of how to use a checklist to document your observation of a science task for third or fourth graders.

Checklist for Science — Grade 3 or 4

Name __Fred Chang__   Date __10-20-93__

TASK: Student will employ the scientific method by making and recording his/her observations during an assigned science task. The task will consist of dissecting an owl pellet and observing and classifying the contents. The student will the discuss the results in a group situation and write about what he/she saw.

Behavior	Observed

Behavior	Poor to Excellent			
	1	2	3	4
Follows directions (Opens owl pellet, removes contents). *Responded to both oral and written directions.*			✓	
Compares contents of owl pellet with illustrations of bones, skulls, etc. *Very thorough*				✓
Classifies and labels findings. *Very thorough — great pleasure in being "scientific."*				✓
Compares and discusses findings with cooperative learning group. *Impatient with slower learners.*	✓			
Makes science journal entry describing experience. *Excellent summary*				✓

Use this checklist to document your observation of a science task for third or fourth graders.

Checklist for Science — Grade 3 or 4

Name _____   Date _____

Task: _____
_____
_____
_____

Behavior	Observed			
	Poor to Excellent			
	1	2	3	4
Follows directions.				
Compares _____ with relevant illustrations.				
Classifies and labels findings.				
Compares and discusses findings with cooperative learning group.				
Makes science journal entry describing experience.				

This is an example of how to use a classroom checklist to compile results from individual checklists.

Classroom Checklist for Task Observation in Science

Grade 3 or 4

Owl Pellets	Follows directions	Compares	Classifies and labels	cooperative group	Journal entry		Comments
Chang, Fred	✓	✓	✓		✓		needs to be more tolerant of others
Garcia, Linda	✓	✓					ESL- great progress!
Moody, Wendy				✓			not much individual effort

Use this classroom checklist to compile results from individual checklists. Run off enough copies to accommodate all the students in your class.

Classroom Checklist for Task Observation in Science
Grade 3 or 4

This is an example of how to use a checklist to document your observation of a science task for fifth or sixth graders.

Checklist for Science

Grade 5 or 6

Name **Chou Tran**   Date **6/1/93**

TASK: Student will use knowledge of science and the scientific method to determine the effect of adding soap to water when attempting to blow the longest-lasting bubbles.

Behavior	Observed			
	Poor to Excellent			
	1	2	3	4
States hypothesis. A solution of water and soap will make longer lasting bubbles and the more soap, the longer the bubbles will last.			✓	
Sets up experiments. Chose 4 beakers. Put measured amounts of water and soap in each. Recorded ratio of soap to water.				✓
Makes and records observations. Blew bubbles and timed how long they lasted. Compiled data into chart.				✓+
Draws a conclusion. " The more soap in a soap and water solution, the longer the bubbles last."				✓
Writes a report documenting experience. Put charts and records into folder. Wrote page describing experiment to put in portfolio.				✓

Use this checklist to document your observation of a science task for fifth or sixth graders.

Checklist for Science

Grade 5 or 6

Name _____   Date _____

Task: _____
_____
_____
_____

Behavior	Observed			
	Poor to Excellent			
	1	2	3	4
States hypothesis.				
Sets up experiments.				
Makes and records observations.				
Draws a conclusion.				
Writes a report documenting experience.				

This is an example of how to use a classroom checklist to compile results from individual checklists.

Classroom Checklist for Task Observation in Science
Grade 5 or 6

Soap Bubbles	States Hypothesis	Sets up experiment	Makes + records observations	Draws Conclusions	Writes/Compiles Report		Comments
Dunstan, Helen	✓	✓-	—	—	—		no sense of organization
Lopez, Conchita							not enough English
Morales, Hector	✓	✓	✓	✓			needs help with report
Tran, Chou	✓	✓	✓+	✓	✓		He really enjoyed this

Use this classroom checklist to compile results from individual checklists. Run off enough copies to accommodate all the students in your class.

Classroom Checklist for Task Observation in Science

Grade 5 or 6

At this grade level the social studies project often takes the form of a simple report designed to introduce students to the fundamentals of gathering and presenting research in a structured form. This is an example of how to use a checklist to keep track of the incremental skills you may want to assess.

Individual Checklist for a Social Studies Project
Grade 1 or 2

Name _Becky Robinson_   Date _9/30/93_

Project _Report on an animal_

Skill	Observed			
	Poor to Excellent			
	1	2	3	4
Skill 1: Chose topic. _Decided to report on tiger_			✓	
Skill 2: Consulted reference book. _Found two books in library. Read with little help._				✓
Skill 3: Wrote about topic. _Put info. into own words. Wrote 1st draft. Edited w/help. Re-copied._				✓
Skill 4: Drew illustration. _Traced picture in book._		✓		
Skill 5: Gave oral report. _Shared information with class. Displayed report. Great job!_				✓

At this grade level the social studies project often takes the form of a simple report designed to introduce students to the fundamentals of gathering and presenting research in a structured form. Decide on the incremental skills you want to assess and use this checklist to keep track of them.

Individual Checklist for a Social Studies Project
Grade 1 or 2

Name _____ Date _____

Project _____

Skill	Observed			
	Poor to Excellent			
	1	2	3	4
Skill 1:				
Skill 2:				
Skill 3:				
Skill 4:				
Skill 5:				

This is an example of how to use a classroom checklist to compile results from individual checklists documenting a social studies project.

Classroom Checklist • Social Studies Project
Grade 1 or 2

Project: Report on an Animal	Skill 1: Topic	Skill 2: Reference	Skill 3: Wrote	Skill 4: Illustration	Skill 5: Oral Report	Skill 6:	Comments
Adamski, Alfred	✓	✓	✓				In progress
Contreras, Rosa	✓	✓		✓			ESL
Miriani, David	✓	✓	✓	✓	✓		Great!
Nguyen, Trang							chicken pox—make-up
Robinson, Becky	✓	✓	✓	✓	✓		Great!
Singer, Elliot							In progress

Use this classroom checklist to compile results from individual checklists documenting a social studies project. Run off enough copies to accommodate all the students in your class.

Classroom Checklist • Social Studies Project
Grade 1 or 2

Project:	Skill 1:	Skill 2:	Skill 3:	Skill 4:	Skill 5:	Skill 6:	Comments

At this grade level the social studies project often takes the form of a more elaborate report designed to introduce students to gathering information from several sources and writing a Table of Contents and Bibliography. A product of some kind may also be required or done for extra credit. This is an example of how to use a checklist to keep track of the incremental skills you may want to assess.

Individual Checklist for a Social Studies Project
Grade 3 or 4

Name _Michelle Hollis_ Date _4/18/93_

Project _American Frontier / Gold Rush_

Skill	Observed
	Poor to Excellent
	1	2	3	4
Skill 1: Information obtained from multiple sources. *Used 6 books according to bibliography*				✓
Skill 2: Format includes Table of Contents and simple Bibliography. *Good TOC / Books listed — not standard form*		✓		
Skill 3: Extras included (folder, cover, illustrations). *No attempt to make a good presentation*	✓			
Skill 4: Oral report given to class. *Excellent oral report*				✓
Skill 5: Completed extra credit work. *Built a model of a covered wagon. Great!*				✓

At this grade level the social studies project often takes the form of a more elaborate report designed to introduce students to gathering information from several sources and writing a Table of Contents and Bibliography. A product of some kind may also be required or done for extra credit. Decide on the incremental skills you want to assess and use this checklist to keep track of them.

Individual Checklist for a Social Studies Project
Grade 3 or 4

Name _____   Date _____

Project _____

Skill	Observed Poor to Excellent			
	1	2	3	4
Skill 1:				
Skill 2:				
Skill 3:				
Skill 4:				
Skill 5:				

This is an example of how to use a classroom checklist to compile results from individual checklists documenting a social studies project.

Classroom Checklist • Social Studies Project
Grade 3 or 4

Project: American Frontier/Gold Rush	Skill 1: Sources	Skill 2: Format	Skill 3: Presentation	Skill 4: Oral Report	Skill 5: Extra Credit	Skill 6:	Comments
Hollis, Michelle	✓	✓	✓	✓	✓		Help with presentation
Mendez, Antonio					✓		ESL
Peck, Margaret	✓			✓			needs writing skills
Prince, Paula	✓	✓	✓	✓	✓		excellent work
Schmitz, Rolf	✓	✓	✓				minimum achievement

Use this classroom checklist to compile results from individual checklists documenting a social studies project. Run off enough copies to accommodate all the students in your class.

Classroom Checklist • Social Studies Project
Grade 3 or 4

Project:	Skill 1:	Skill 2:	Skill 3:	Skill 4:	Skill 5:	Skill 6:	Comments

At this grade level the social studies project often takes the form of a more elaborate report designed to reinforce the idea of gathering information from several sources and writing a Table of Contents and Bibliography. Alternatively, it may focus entirely on the production of a creative product that will embody all of the research in an attractive form. This is an example of how to use a checklist to keep track of the incremental skills you may want to assess.

Individual Checklist for a Social Studies Project
Grade 5 or 6

Name _Karen Mahoney_   Date _5/25/93_

Project _Report on country in form of travel brochure_

Skill	Observed			
	Poor to Excellent			
	1	2	3	4
Skill 1: Information obtained from multiple sources. *Bibliography shows 7 sources*			✓	
Skill 2: Product meets requirements. — facts (population, area, location, climate, etc.) — areas (housing, food, lifestyle, etc.) *All info included*				✓
Skill 3: Extras included (cover, illustrations, etc.). *Beautifully put-together brochure*				✓
Skill 4: Oral report given to class. *Karen has trouble speaking to a group*		✓		
Skill 5: Completed extra credit work. *Obtained travel posters*				✓

At this grade level the social studies project often takes the form of a more elaborate report designed to reinforce the idea of gathering information from several sources and writing a Table of Contents and Bibliography. Alternatively, it may focus entirely on the production of a creative product that will embody all of the research in an attractive form. Decide on the incremental skills you want to assess and use this checklist to keep track of them.

Individual Checklist for a Social Studies Project
Grade 5 or 6

Name _____   Date _____

Project _____

Skill	Observed			
	Poor to Excellent			
	1	2	3	4
Skill 1:				
Skill 2:				
Skill 3:				
Skill 4:				
Skill 5:				

This is an example of how to use a classroom checklist to compile results from individual checklists documenting a social studies project.

Classroom Checklist ▪ Social Studies Project
Grade 5 or 6

Project: Country Report/ Travel Brochure	Skill 1: Sources	Skill 2: Requirements	Skill 3: Extras	Skill 4: Oral Reports	Skill 5: Extra Credit	Skill 6:	Comments
Astor, Trevor		✓	✓	✓			no biblio
Johnson, Leon	✓	✓	✓	✓			Good job!
Mahoney, Karen	✓	✓	✓	✓	✓		Help with public speaking
Wallace, Shanice	✓	✓	✓				Make up oral report

Use this classroom checklist to compile results from individual checklists documenting a social studies project. Run off enough copies to accommodate all the students in your class.

Classroom Checklist ▪ Social Studies Project
Grade 5 or 6

Project:	Skill 1:	Skill 2:	Skill 3:	Skill 4:	Skill 5:	Skill 6:	Comments

This is an example of how to use a checklist to document your observation of your students' use of the thinking skills (based on Bloom's Taxonomy).

Checklist for the Thinking Skills
(Based on Bloom)
Example of Topic at Grade 1 or 2

Name _Peter Gregory_   Date _10-17-93_

Task _Discussing Assembly Rules — Before and After_

Demonstrated	How
Knowledge	Answered questions such as "What is an assembly?" and "Have we been to one before?"
Comprehension	Own words: "We go to the cafeteria and see a program with the other kids."
Application	Showed how to sit at an assembly.
Analysis	Knew <u>why</u> we are quiet at an assembly: "to hear."
Synthesis	Generated helpful ideas: "We can keep our hands to ourselves."
Evaluation	Discussed how we acted as measured by above criteria.

This is an example of how to use a checklist to document your observation of your students' use of the thinking skills (based on Bloom's Taxonomy).

Checklist for the Thinking Skills

(Based on Bloom)

Example of Topic at Grade 3 or 4

Name _Bianca Garcia_   Date _2/4/93_

Task _Open-ended math problem (Best graph to use)_

Demonstrated	How
Knowledge	Knew different graphs — named bar, line, circle, and pictograph
Comprehension	Stated that graphs help people "see" information
Application	Made two graphs using info to try methods
Analysis	Decided which graph to use
Synthesis	Used Application and Analysis (above) to produce a product that worked
Evaluation	Discussed product telling why it was best for given data

This is an example of how to use a checklist to document your observation of your students' use of the thinking skills (based on Bloom's Taxonomy).

Checklist for the Thinking Skills

(Based on Bloom)

Example of Topic at Grade 5 or 6

Name _Alice van Helsing_ Date _12-20-93_

Task _Discuss Ethnic Holiday Celebrations_

Demonstrated	How
Knowledge	Has general info about different ethnic customs
Comprehension	States: "Ways to celebrate are based on family traditions."
Application	Talks about different customs celebrated by her neighbors
Analysis	Compares/contrasts customs
Synthesis	Invents new celebration that reflects classroom culture
Evaluation	Enters into discussion that attempts to clarify idea that there is no "best" way to celebrate.

Use this checklist to document your observation of your students' use of the thinking skills (based on Bloom's Taxonomy) as applied to a topic of your choice.

Checklist for the Thinking Skills

(Based on Bloom)

Name _____   Date _____

Task _____

Demonstrated	How
Knowledge	
Comprehension	
Application	
Analysis	
Synthesis	
Evaluation	

This is an example of how to use a classroom checklist to compile results from individual checklists documenting the thinking skills.

Classroom Checklist • Thinking Skills

Discussing Assembly rules — Before and After	Knowledge	Comprehension	Application	Analysis	Synthesis	Evaluation	Comments
Bosch, Jeremy	✓		✓			✓	
Vegas, Pamela						✓	1st Assembly
Fontes, Julio	✓	✓				✓	
Gregory, Peter	✓	✓	✓	✓	✓	✓	Very alert
Juarez, Rosita			✓				Just coming to English

Use this classroom checklist to compile results from individual checklist documenting the thinking skills. Run off enough copies to accommodate all the students in your class.

Classroom Checklist • Thinking Skills

Task:	Knowledge	Comprehension	Application	Analysis	Synthesis	Evaluation	Comments

Portfolios:
What, How, When, and Why

What Is Portfolio Assessment?

Portfolio assessment is a system of gathering relevant samples of a student's work in order to document his or her educational progress.

Although portfolio assessment still qualifies as part of the "new" assessment, it has been around long enough to become generally accepted (not so scary anymore), and to have undergone some changes and modifications of its own.

You can tell that portfolio assessment has become generally accepted because articles in educational journals and teachers publications no longer include long detailed explanations about it every time it is mentioned. They just say "portfolio assessment" and take it for granted that it is well in place in the educational system. This may be true. Teachers have certainly heard of it. Many of them have implemented the process in their classrooms. Just as many, however, have heard of it and rejected it. A quick review may help some of those who said "No, thanks!" to take another look.

Portfolio assessment is really not as scary as it used to be because of all the people who have tried it and liked it. It has turned out to be not so hard as it looked at first. It has benefits that far outweigh the time it takes to set it motion. Students and parents like it, and it makes a classroom more fun.

Unfortunately, the fact that portfolio assessment is generally accepted and less scary is being offset to some degree by the changes and modifications it is undergoing. Also, some of the misuses and abuses that teachers were warned about have begun to creep into the process. Districts have begun to control the material that must be kept in a portfolio, and student privacy and ownership are not always respected.

However, a great many of the problems people have with portfolios are the result of name changes. The names for things change constantly in education. This probably happens because people do not want to be accused of using the ideas that were originated by others. Nevertheless, it can be confusing. Perhaps we should adopt more generic names. For example, the portfolio that could be described as "the portfolio that is begun at the start of the year and consists of a great deal of miscellaneous work" is often referred to as a Collection Portfolio, an Accumulation Portfolio, and an Initial Portfolio. "The portfolio that results from choosing samples of a student's work in order to show achievement or progress" is sometimes called a Showcase Portfolio, a Display Portfolio, or a Semester Portfolio. In case of confusion, read the description and skip over the trendy name!

Portfolios:
What, How, When, and Why *(cont.)*

What are Portfolios?

Portfolios can be thought of in two ways — as containers for the work students do and as part of a unique assessment method which allows for reflection on student achievement and growth.

If you think of portfolios as containers, you will use them to hold all of the writing samples and reports, rubrics, and checklists generated by your students during the year. This is a legitimate and very useful portfolio function.

If you think of portfolios as part of a unique assessment method, you will still put everything in them, including the things listed above plus reading logs, contracts, and anecdotal records. However, you go one or two steps further. You will also use these materials as a basis for reflection by both the teacher and the students themselves.

How Do You Put Portfolios into Action?

The following steps will help you to establish and implement a system of portfolio assessment in your classroom.

1. Make a container (anything from a folded piece of construction paper to a sturdy cardboard box) for each student and label it with his or her name.

2. Find an accessible (for you and the students) area in your classroom to place these containers.

3. Decide what you want to keep. In a thematic classroom you may decide, for example, to keep samples that illustrate your theme in each curriculum area. You may want to add anecdotal records and checklists of one kind or another.

Important• Important • Important • Important • Important • Important

Every piece of paper in the portfolio must be dated!!!

---

4. Set up a system for filing. Each student may be responsible for getting his or her own papers into the portfolio, or a Portfolio Monitor may be responsible for filing everything. If you decide to have a Portfolio Monitor, make sure he or she trains a back-up. Even Portfolio Monitors get sick, and papers pile up quickly!

Portfolios:
What, How, When, and Why *(cont.)*

5. Pick a time to sort the papers. In a thematic classroom this might be at the end of a short unit or at a good stopping point in a long unit. Pass out the portfolios and have the students choose papers according to a set of criteria that suits your purpose. For example, you might have them choose:

- a reading checklist

- a sample of creative writing

- a related math paper

- a research paper in social studies

These papers should now be moved into a Showcase Portfolio (see page 129), the remaining papers should go home, the empty portfolios should be returned to the accessible area, and you are ready to start over again.

6. At report card and/or conference time — if you dated all of the papers! — you will be ready and able to look through the Showcase Portfolios and assess the progress of the students. You will also be able to back up your assessments with examples that will substantiate your judgments. This is the real plus for the teacher in portfolio assessment.

7. By the end of the semester or the school year, students will have a rich record of their achievement for the year. Besides providing a wonderful boost for self-esteem, the completed portfolio will be a proud display for Open House and a great memory-enhancer for the grade just completed.

When Should You Use Portfolios?

Portfolios can be used at any grade level, in any kind of classroom, for any variety of subject matter.

A new and exciting alternative use of portfolio assessment is to assist teachers in evaluating their own teaching methods and materials. Many teacher-training programs ask student teachers to build portfolios of their teaching units for the purpose of reflecting on their own experiences. These materials can then be clarified or elaborated upon with the benefit of hindsight.

Any teacher can build this kind of a portfolio, eliminating the need to undergo unpleasant teaching experiences more than once or to reinvent the perfect plan. Notations can be made about shortcuts and supplementary materials, sources and resources, what worked and what did not — "That was great!" and "I'll never try that again!" You will find some helpful forms for this kind of portfolio use at the end of this book.

Portfolios:
What, How, When, and Why *(cont.)*

Why Should You Use Portfolios?

- Portfolios help the students

    — become self-aware learners.

    — become observers of and participants in their own academic growth.

    — claim ownership of their own learning.

- Portfolios help the teachers

    — record, store, and access important information.

    — evaluate student progress.

    — produce evidence for grades.

    — look at the effectiveness of their own teaching.

Are There Some Forms I Can Use?

On the following pages you will find some handy forms — filled out as examples and blank for you to run off and use — for use in portfolio assessment. There are forms for anecdotal records, reading and writing logs, contracts, and all kinds of reflections. There are also useful forms for communicating with parents about your assessment process as well as forms that will help you to build a portfolio of your own.

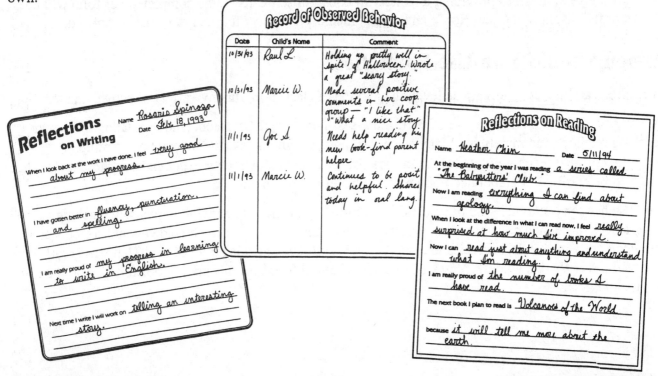

Portfolios In Action

Sectional Table of Contents

What's In It? — Writing Process

Run off this form and staple it on top of a writing process packet. Check off the relevant items and add the packet to the portfolio.

- -

The Writing Process

This packet contains the following items:

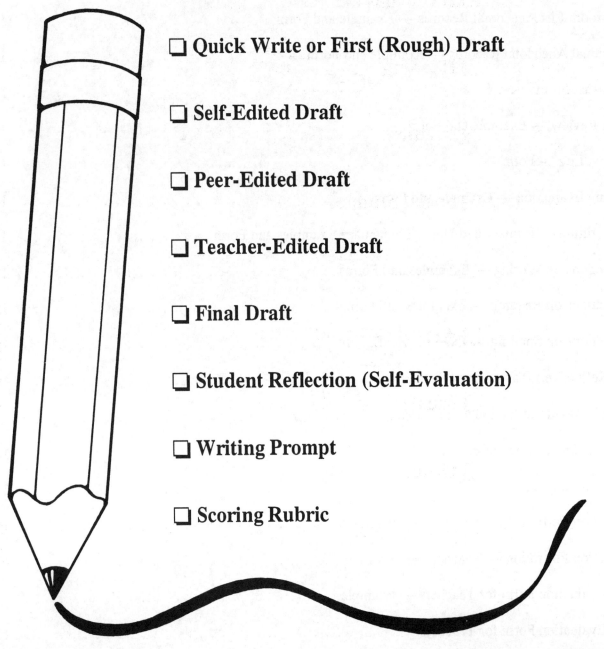

❑ **Quick Write or First (Rough) Draft**

❑ **Self-Edited Draft**

❑ **Peer-Edited Draft**

❑ **Teacher-Edited Draft**

❑ **Final Draft**

❑ **Student Reflection (Self-Evaluation)**

❑ **Writing Prompt**

❑ **Scoring Rubric**

What's In It? — Thematic Unit

Run off this form and attach it to the work that represents a thematic unit you have included in the portfolio. If the whole portfolio is devoted to one theme, attach this form to the cover — inside or outside. List the items you have chosen to save.

Our Thematic Unit on _____

This packet contains the following items:

- ❏ **Reading**

- ❏ **Writing**

- ❏ **Social Studies**

- ❏ **Science**

- ❏ **Art**

- ❏ **Music**

- ❏ **Other**

- ❏ **Student Reflection on Work**

What's In It? — Collection Portfolio

Attach this form or a variation of it to the inside front cover of each Collection Portfolio so interested people will know what they are looking at. Save yourself hours of individual explanations by listing pieces of work in the appropriate categories as they are placed in the portfolio. You can do this for younger children; older students can list their own.

- -

This Collection Portfolio

belongs to _____

It contains samples of my work in these subject areas:

❑ **Writing**

❑ **Mathematics**

❑ **Social Studies**

❑ **Science**

❑ **Art/Music**

❑ **Other**

What's In It? — Showcase Portfolio

You can attach this form to the front cover of each student's Showcase Portfolio. It makes a statement about progress as well as giving information about the contents of the portfolio itself.

- -

This Showcase Portfolio

belongs to _____

Start from the back —

Things from last September.

I was little then —

Remember?

Read toward the front

And you will see

Just how big

I'm getting to be!

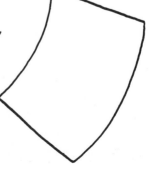

Anecdotal Records and the New Assessment

Old-Style Anecdotal Records

Anecdotal records used to be lists kept by teachers who were trying to document behavior problems that were disrupting their classrooms. They were lists of comments stated factually and objectively without teacher interpretation or judgment. They were designed to stand alone.

11/22 Johnny fell out of his chair five times before lunch.

11/23 Johnny hit Mary when he walked by her chair to go to recess.

11/24 Johnny called the yard-duty teacher "a dork" when she asked him to wait in line for a drink.

11/24 Johnny ripped up his spelling test when he couldn't remember how to spell a word.

Armed with this list, the teacher would ask the principal or the school counselor for help in dealing with a difficult child.

New-Style Anecdotal Records

Although the old-style anecdotal record may still exist, the term anecdotal record has been transferred into the realm of portfolio assessment and has taken on a new meaning.

Anecdotal records, new-style, are positive comments that document the development and growth of children. They depend on teacher interpretation and judgment and deal with what children can do, not what they cannot do. They may deal with interactions between children and their schoolwork or interactions between children and other children or children and adults.

12/5 Melody wrote a story by herself using invented spelling. She then read the story to the class.

12/7 Melody played handball without getting into a fight today. She waited in line for her turn and was able to accept being called "out" when she missed the ball.

12/8 Melody wrote a story about the rain. She used spelling words and was able to transfer her knowledge of how to spell the words to her original writing.

Comments like this are kept on lists of one kind or another and then filed in portfolios. Some teachers like to keep running lists including many students and then transfer these comments to a notebook with pages for each individual child. The teacher can flip to the appropriate page and make an entry. When a page is filled up, it can be filed in the child's portfolio and a new page with that child's name inserted in the notebook. Forms that support both of these methods follow.

Classroom List
Anecdotal Records — Example

This is an example of how to keep a running classroom list of observed behaviors. The comments are written with the idea of being transferred to individual forms, and maybe elaborated upon, at the end of the day.

Record of Observed Behavior

Date	Child's Name	Comment
10/31/93	Raul L.	Holding up pretty well in spite of Halloween! Wrote a great "scary story."
10/31/93	Marcie W.	Made several positive comments in her coop. group — "I like that" and "What a nice story."
11/1/93	Joe S.	Needs help reading his new book—find parent helper
11/1/93	Marcie W.	Continues to be positive and helpful. Shared today in oral lang.

Classroom List
Anecdotal Records — Form

Run off some of these classroom lists and carry them around on a clipboard to make moment-by-moment comments on what you observe in your classroom. Transfer the information to individual record forms at the end of the day.

Record of Observed Behavior

Date	Child's Name	Comment

Individual Anecdotal Records — Example

This is an example of how to keep an individual record of observed behaviors. One of these pages are made for each student and kept in alphabetical order for convenient access in a three-ring binder. When the page is filled up, it can be replaced with a new page and the filled page placed in the student's portfolio.

Individual Anecdotal Record

Name _Marcie Wallace_

Date	Comment
10/15/93	Having trouble with group skills— we talked about strategies she could try. I suggested some positive comments.
10/31/93	Marcie made several positive comments in her cooperative group today — "I like that" and "What a nice story."
11/1/93	Continues to be positive and helpful — shared today in oral language.

Individual Anecdotal Record — Form

Run off a stack of these forms and keep them — one for each student in your class — in a three-ring binder. Make your notes right on the appropriate form. When a page is filled up, it can be replaced with a new page and the filled page placed in the student's portfolio. No time is lost transcribing information!

Individual Anecdotal Record

Name _____

Date	Comment

Book List Form — Grade 1 or 2

Run off copies of this form for your students. They can use them at home and return them when they are filled up to be placed in their portfolios. Or they can keep them in their portfolios and update them when they finish a book. Or they can have two at a time — one for home use and one for use at school. Parents can verify home reading by initialing the book entry. Decide on a quick rating system — maybe 1 to 5 stars or happy faces. Kids love to rate their reading.

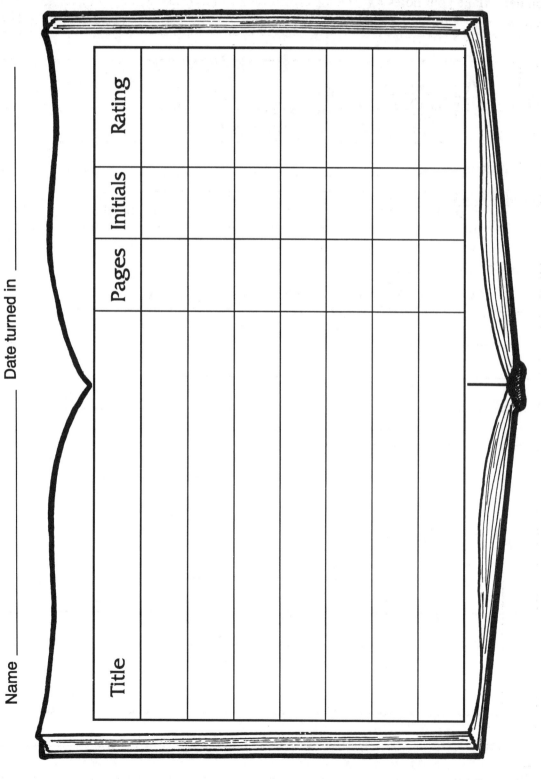

Books I Have Read

Name _____

Date turned in _____

Title	Pages	Initials	Rating

Book Review Form — Example

You may want your students to report in depth on the books they read — at least some of them. This form will give them more scope for expressing opinions. You might post these reviews as a device to motivate other students to read books their classmates liked. This is an example of how one of these forms might be used.

Name _Mike Andrews_   Date _1/18_

Book Review

Title _Alexander_

Author _Judith Viorst_

Illustrator _____

Number of Pages _____

This book was about

a very bad day

I (☒ liked, ☐ didn't like) this book because

it was funny.

Book Review — Form

You can run off copies of this form for your students to use to report on the books they read during the school year.

Name _____   Date _____

Book Review

Title _____

Author _____

Illustrator _____

Number of Pages _____

This book was about

_____

_____

_____

_____

_____

_____

I (☐ liked, ☐ didn't like) this book because

_____

_____

_____

_____

_____

_____

Writing Log — Form

Run off copies of this form for your students. They can use them to keep track of their writing assignments as they complete them. Store them in the portfolios for individual access and updating.

Assignment	Draft 1	Draft 2	Draft 3	Final Draft

Writing Evaluation — Example

This is an example of how a form can be used to help a student keep a running evaluation of an individual assignment. You can add to or replace the points to be considered to suit your own areas of focus in writing. Readers can initial and date the appropriate squares. Help younger students to read and fill in the squares as a step toward independent record-keeping.

Evaluation Form

Name *Missy Davila*   Date *added to portfolio on 12/10/93*

Assignment *Persuasive essay — We should Have a Soft Drink Machine at School*

		Author	Partner	Teacher
Clarity	The reader can understand what I am trying to say.	yes	Yes	*good editing job!*
	My reasons are logical.	yes	Mostly	
	I am writing to my audience.	needs to be more formal	Okay now	
Conventions	I used capital letters correctly.	✓	✓	✓
	I used punctuation correctly.	✓	check commas	okay now
	My spelling is phonetic in the early drafts and corrected in the final drafts.	✓	✓	✓
	My handwriting can be read easily.	✓	✓	✓
Writing Process	I have read and edited my work.	yes	—	—
	My writing partner has read and edited my work.	yes	Yes	—
	The teacher has read and edited my work.	yes	—	*MP*

Writing Evaluation — Form

Use this form to help a student keep a running evaluation of an individual assignment. You can add to or replace the points to be considered to suit your own areas of focus in writing. Readers can initial and date the appropriate squares. Help younger students to read and fill in the squares as a step toward independent record-keeping.

Evaluation Form

Name _____   Date _____

Assignment _____

		Author	Partner	Teacher
Clarity	The reader can understand what I am trying to say.			
	My reasons are logical.			
	I am writing to my audience.			
Conventions	I used capital letters correctly.			
	I used punctuation correctly.			
	My spelling is phonetic in the early drafts and corrected in the final drafts.			
	My handwriting can be read easily.			
Writing Process	I have read and edited my work.			
	My writing partner has read and edited my work.			
	The teacher has read and edited my work.			

Writing Evaluation — Peer Editing Form

Primary Example

This is an example of how a student in the primary grades might use this form to respond after reading the work of another student. (Very young students could dictate responses, and the teacher could write them.) Ask students to make only positive comments.

- -

Writing Evaluation — Peer Editing Form

Reader's Name ___Tracy Lenihan___   Date ___Feb. 15, 1993___

Author's Name ___Shaneequa Johnson___

Title of Piece ___All About Lincoln___

This piece of writing was ___intrusting.___

_____

It made me feel ___happy.___

_____

The part I liked best was ___about the log cabin.___

_____

Next time the author might want to work on ___I don't no.___

_____

Writing Evaluation —
Peer Editing Form

Upper Elementary Example

This is an example of how a student in the upper elementary grades might use this form to respond after reading the work of another student. Ask students to make only positive comments.

- -

Writing Evaluation — Peer Editing Form

Reader's Name __Ron Churchill__   Date __3/14/93__

Author's Name __Holly Nguyen__

Title of Piece __Looking Forward To Spring__

This piece of writing was __very descriptive. There were__ __lots of words that made me see pictures.__

It made me feel __good to read it.__

The part I liked best was __all of it. I can't decide.__

Next time the author might want to work on __a different kind of__ __writing. She's already good at this kind.__

Writing Evaluation —
Peer Editing Form *(cont.)*

Ask your students to fill out this form (or one like it) after reading the work of another student. Younger students may respond with a symbol such as a happy face. Ask students to make only positive comments.

Writing Evaluation — Peer Editing Form

Reader's Name_____   Date_____

Author's Name _____

Title of Piece_____

This piece of writing was _____

_____

It made me feel _____

_____

The part I liked best was _____

_____

Next time the author might want to work on _____

_____

Reflections on Writing — Primary Example

This is an example of how to use a form to help students start the process of reflecting on their own writing. This particular form was designed for primary children and requires little writing. If your students need a more sophisticated form, use the one for upper elementary students that follows. Allow plenty of time to look over the work that is being reflected upon. When the form is completed, attach it to the work and include it in the student's portfolio.

- -

Reflections on Writing

Name _Jan Manden_   Date _Jan. 10, 1993_

When I look back at the work I have done, I feel

☺ 😐 ☹

I have gotten better in   ⟨writing sentences,⟩

⟨using capitals and periods,⟩

spelling,

⟨telling a story,⟩

telling my ideas about something.

I am really proud of

my Stories.

_____

Next time I write I will

Work on Speling.

Reflections on Writing — Primary Form

Run off copies of this form for your students to use as they start the process of reflecting on their own writing. This particular form was designed for primary children and requires little writing. If your students need a more sophisticated form, use the one for upper elementary students that follows. Allow plenty of time to look over the work that is being reflected upon. When the form is completed, attach it to the work and include it in the student's portfolio.

- -

Reflections on Writing

Name _____   Date _____

When I look back at the work I have done, I feel

I have gotten better in   writing sentences.

using capitals and periods.

spelling.

telling a story.

telling my ideas about something.

I am really proud of

_____

_____

Next time I write I will

_____

_____

Reflections on Writing — Upper Elementary Example

This is an example of how to use a form to help students start the process of reflecting on their own writing. (Although this form was designed for upper elementary children, it could be used by younger children if the teacher reads it to them and briefly records their answers. Some primary students may, of course, be ready to use it alone.) Allow plenty of time to look over the work that is being reflected upon. When the form is completed, attach it to the work and include it in the student's portfolio.

- -

Reflections on Writing

Name _Rosario Spinoza_

Date _Feb. 18, 1993_

When I look back at the work I have done, I feel _very good about my progress._

I have gotten better in _fluency, punctuation, and spelling._

I am really proud of _my progress in learning to write in English._

Next time I write I will work on _telling an interesting story._

Reflections on Writing — Upper Elementary Form

Run off copies of this form for your students to use as they start the process of reflecting on their own writing. (Although this form was designed for upper elementary children, it could be used by younger children if the teacher reads it to them and briefly records their answers. Some primary students may, of course, be ready to use it alone.) Allow plenty of time to look over the work that is being reflected upon. When the form is completed, attach it to the work and include it in the student's portfolio.

Reflections on Writing

Name _____

Date _____

When I look back at the work I have done, I feel _____

_____

_____

_____

I have gotten better in _____

_____

_____

_____

I am really proud of _____

_____

_____

_____

Next time I write I will work on _____

_____

_____

Reflections on Reading — Primary Example

This is an example of how to use a form to help students start the process of reflecting on their own progress in reading. This particular form was designed for primary children and requires little writing. A teacher/student conference affords a good time to start reflecting on progress in reading. At that time the teacher can help the student fill in the name of the book he or she was reading at the beginning of the year.

Reflections on Reading

Name **Thanh Duong**   Date **4/18/93**

At the beginning of the year, I was reading **Watch the Wind**

Now I am reading **Wake the Sun**

This is how I feel about my progress in reading:

☺ 😐 ☹

I am really proud of _____

_____

_____

_____

Note Thanh needs help in reading and in self-esteem.

The next book I plan to read is **Something easy**

_____

Reflections on Reading — Primary Form

Run off copies of this form for your students to use as they start the process of reflecting on their own progress in reading. This particular form was designed for primary children and requires little writing. A teacher/student conference affords a good time to start reflecting on progress in reading. At that time the teacher can help the student fill in the name of the book he or she was reading at the beginning of the year.

Reflections on Reading

Name _____   Date_____

At the beginning of the year, I was reading _____

Now I am reading _____

This is how I feel about my progress in reading:

◯   ◯   ◯

I am really proud of_____

_____

_____

_____

The next book I plan to read is _____

_____

Reflections on Reading — Upper Elementary Example

This is an example of how to use a form to help students start the process of reflecting on their own progress in reading. Teacher/student conferences afford a good opportunity for this. At that time the teacher can help the students decide on the books they will read next.

- -

Reflections on Reading

Name _Heather Chin_   Date _5/11/94_

At the beginning of the year I was reading _a series called "The Babysitters' Club."_

Now I am reading _everything I can find about geology._

When I look at the difference in what I can read now, I feel _really surprised at how much I've improved._

Now I can _read just about anything and understand what I'm reading._

I am really proud of _the number of books I have read._

The next book I plan to read is _Volcanoes of the World_

because _it will tell me more about the earth._

Reflections on Reading — Upper Elementary Form

Run off copies of this form for your students to use as they start the process of reflecting on their own progress in reading. Teacher/student conferences afford a good opportunity for this. At that time the teacher can help the students decide on the books they will read next.

- -

Reflections on Reading

Name _____ Date _____

At the beginning of the year I was reading _____
_____

Now I am reading _____
_____

When I look at the difference in what I can read now, I feel _____
_____

Now I can _____
_____

I am really proud of _____
_____

The next book I plan to read is _____
_____

because _____
_____

Reflections on Spelling — Primary Example

This is an example of how to use a form to help students start the process of reflecting on their own progress in spelling. Spelling — especially invented or estimated (phonetic) spelling — is being mentioned more and more often as an indicator of a student's control of the language. This particular form was designed for primary students and requires little writing. A teacher/student conference affords a good time to start reflecting on progress in spelling.

- -

Reflections on Spelling

Name _Peter Rubens_   Date _4/2/93_

This is how I feel about my progress in spelling:

☺ ☺ ☹

I have learned to spell many words the way they are spelled in books. Here are some words I can spell:

I	am	Was
look	read	to

When I don't know how to spell a word, I can

Sound it out

ask the teacher

It is fun to be able to spell because

it helps you write.

Reflections on Spelling — Primary Form

Run off copies of this form for your students to use as they start the process of reflecting on their own progress in spelling. Spelling — especially invented or estimated (phonetic) spelling — is being mentioned more and more often as an indicator of a student's control of the language. This particular form was designed for primary students and requires little writing. A teacher/student conference affords a good time to start reflecting on progress in spelling.

- -

Reflections on Spelling

Name _____   Date _____

This is how I feel about my progress in spelling:

☺   😐   ☹

I have learned to spell many words the way they are spelled in books. Here are some words I can spell:

_____   _____   _____

_____   _____   _____

_____   _____   _____

When I don't know how to spell a word, I can

_____

_____

It is fun to be able to spell because

_____

Reflections on Spelling — Upper Elementary Example

This is an example of how to use a form to help students start the process of reflecting on their own progress in spelling. Spelling — especially invented or estimated (phonetic) spelling — is being mentioned more and more often as an indicator of a student's control of the language. A teacher/student conference affords a good time to start reflecting on progress in spelling.

Reflections on Spelling

Name _Tonya Kravitz_   Date _3/18/93_

When I compare my spelling at the beginning of the year to my spelling now, I see that I have learned to spell many words the way they are spelled in books. Here are some words I can spell:

thought   _separate_   _neighbor_

there   _their_   _they're_

When I don't know how to spell a word, I can

look in the dictionary

sound out the word

run the spell-check on the computer

It is important to know how to sound words out because

it helps me be fluent in my writing.

It is important to learn conventional "book" spelling because

other people can read what I write.

Reflections on Spelling — Upper Elementary Form

Run off copies of this form for your students to use as they start the process of reflecting on their own progress in spelling. Spelling — especially invented or estimated (phonetic) spelling — is being mentioned more and more often as an indicator of a student's control of the language. A teacher/student conference affords a good time to start reflecting on progress in spelling.

Reflections on Spelling

Name _____   Date _____

When I compare my spelling at the beginning of the year to my spelling now, I see that I have learned to spell many words the way they are spelled in books. Here are some words I can spell:

_____   _____   _____

_____   _____   _____

_____   _____   _____

When I don't know how to spell a word, I can

_____

_____

_____

It is important to know how to sound words out because

_____

_____

It is important to learn conventional "book" spelling because

_____

_____

The Reflective Essay — Teacher Script

Although students can be helped to reflect upon their progress by filling out a loosely structured form (see preceding pages), the best reflections are in an even less structured form. Older students can write this reflection on their own. Younger students can reflect orally, and you, the teacher, can write down their comments.

Take time to explain and brainstorm examples of the qualities you want the students to look for in their writing.

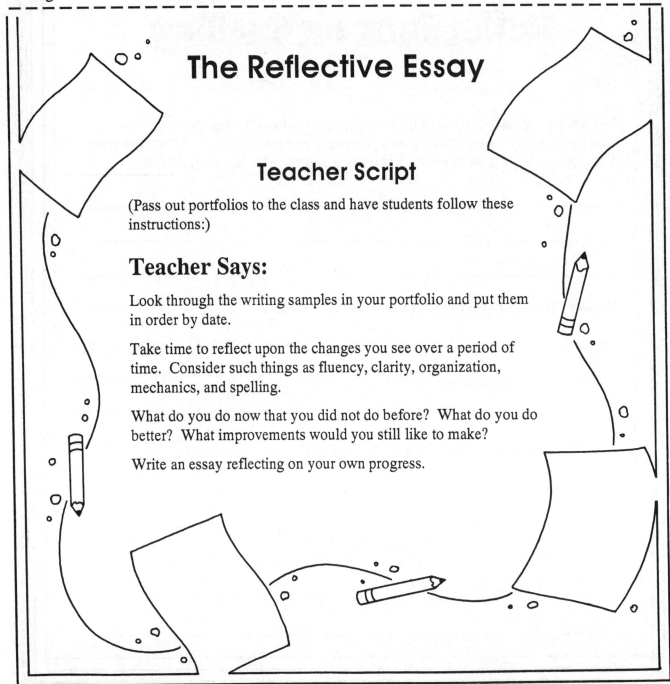

The Reflective Essay

Teacher Script

(Pass out portfolios to the class and have students follow these instructions:)

Teacher Says:

Look through the writing samples in your portfolio and put them in order by date.

Take time to reflect upon the changes you see over a period of time. Consider such things as fluency, clarity, organization, mechanics, and spelling.

What do you do now that you did not do before? What do you do better? What improvements would you still like to make?

Write an essay reflecting on your own progress.

The Reflective Essay — Student Prompt

Look through the writing samples in your portfolio and put them in order by date.

Take time to reflect upon the changes you see over a period of time. Consider such things as fluency, clarity, organization, mechanics, and spelling.

What do you now that you did not do before? What do you do better? What improvements would you still like to make?

Write an essay reflecting on your own progress.

_____

_____

_____

_____

_____

_____

_____

_____

_____

_____

_____

_____

_____

_____

_____

Portfolios —
Introduction to the Parents

If you are going to use portfolio assessment in your classroom, it is a good idea to let parents know what to expect because there are some significant differences between the portfolio assessment classroom and the conventional classroom. These differences will not upset parents if they know about them and expect them in advance. You might want to copy this letter and send it home or make a variation of your own. Do not forget to get your principal's okay, if that is a requirement in your school.

Dear Parents,

This year I will be using Portfolio Assessment in my classroom. This is a system in which the students' work is collected in personal folders and saved for the purpose of evaluating progress. This system is not only educationally beneficial for the students; it is also fun. It gives the students the feeling that they have control of their own learning.

Portfolio assessment is particularly suitable for assessing growth in a classroom using cooperative learning groups and the writing process. We will be using both of those strategies together with thematic units that should pull all of the different curriculum areas together for your student.

I will explain this system in detail at Back-to-School Night and at our first conference, but in the meantime I want to give you some information that will eliminate some possible concerns.

- Not as much daily work will be coming home.

  — Work will be saved in the portfolios.

  — You will get the work to take home at conference time and/or at the end of the year.

  — A great deal of our classroom learning experience will take place through discussion in cooperative groups.

- "Invented" or phonetic spelling will be encouraged as part of the writing process.

Please feel free to come in and visit to see all of these exciting innovations in action. If you cannot come in, collect your questions for Back-to-School Night, and I will try to answer them then.

Sincerely,

Portfolio Presentation to Parents

Parent involvement in portfolio assessment is "in." One way to achieve this goal and still hold on to your own control of the assessment process is to introduce the Portfolio Presentation. There are two kinds: in-school and at-home. Some teachers are arranging Portfolio Afternoons or even Portfolio Evenings when parents come and listen to oral presentations and then view the portfolios. Those students whose parents cannot attend may take their portfolios home and make their presentations there. In either case, parents are asked to fill out a form responding to the portfolio and the presentation and return it to the teacher.

- -

Portfolio Presentation Form for Parents

Student's Name _____

Presented To _____

Date _____

Parents: After your child has given the portfolio presentation, please take a few minutes to complete this form and return it to the teacher.

Did you notice any evidence of

_____ improvement or growth? (Note dates.)

_____ imagination/creativity?

_____ thinking skills?

_____ ability to rewrite, revise, correct mistakes?

_____ self-evaluation (comments, reflection on work)?

_____ cooperative group skills?

_____ organizational ability?

_____ positive attitude?

_____ ability to compute?

_____ more control of conventional spelling?

Did you understand your child's explanation during the oral presentation? How good is his/her ability to communicate?

_____

_____

_____

Parent's Signature: _____

Portfolios at Home

Parents can sometimes be persuaded to support your portfolio assessment program if they are encouraged to start a portfolio for their child at home. Then they share the fun, and they also experience the benefits. You might introduce the idea with a letter like this.

Dear Parents,

Since we are building portfolios at school, I thought you might like to share the fun and at the same time build a lasting keepsake by making a Home Portfolio for your child.

1. Get your child a folder of some kind. Save things the child is particularly proud of — a drawing, a letter written to a grandparent, a photograph, or an award. If something has been up on the refrigerator door for a long time, it can move into the portfolio and make room for something new.

2. Encourage your child to talk about the things selected for the portfolio. Why did he or she select it? What special meaning does it have?

3. Write down your child's comments or have a child who is old enough write a sentence or two explaining his or her choice and include the comments in the portfolio.

4. Have your child write comments over a period of time about changes seen in the items added to the portfolio: quality of writing, spelling, and so on.

I hope you enjoy this activity with your child and continue it through the years.

Sincerely,

Collection Portfolios
for Teachers — Example

This is an example of how teachers can take advantage of portfolios for documenting and evaluating their own professional growth. When you create a unit, pop it into a manila envelope along with all the associated materials — masters, book lists, snapshots of projects and bulletin boards — and put it into a portfolio of your own. Your "portfolio" might be a cupboard or a filing cabinet. Attach a form like this to the inside of the front cover and keep track of what you have.

Classroom Collection Portfolio

Unit	Date	Success?	Changes?
Dinosaurs	9/25/92	yes	Needs additional worksheets
Weather	10/15/92	so so	spark up or abandon!
Thanksgiving	11/25/92	yes	Needs more puzzles, etc.
World Holidays	12/18/92	NO!	Find new unit on this subject.

Collection Portfolios
for Teachers — Form

This is a copy of the form demonstrated on page 169. You can run it off and use it in your own portfolio.

Classroom Collection Portfolio

Unit	Date	Success?	Changes?

Unit Evaluation Form
for Teachers — Example

This is an example of how to use an evaluation form when you create a unit as described on the preceding pages. Staple this form to the outside of the manila envelope before you place the unit and its associated materials in.

- -

Unit Evaluation Form for Teachers

Unit _World Holidays_　　Date Used _December_

Instructional Goals: _Writing/Reading/Math all addressed as well as social studies_

Assessment Strategies: _Rubrics included in packet Checklists " " "_

Associated Projects: _Cookie Cook Book Cookie Party_

Books/Materials Needed: _More cookie recipes for next year_

Bulletin Board Ideas: _See snapshots enclosed_

Worksheets: _Black-line masters_

Evaluation of Unit:

_____ Great!　　__✓__ Good　　_____ So-So　　_____ Never Again!

Comments:
Replace old material with this unit.

Unit Evaluation Form
for Teachers

Use this evaluation form when you create a unit of your own. Fill out this form and staple it to the outside of the manilla envelope before you place the unit and its associated materials in it.

Unit Evaluation Form for Teachers

Unit _____ Date Used _____

Instructional Goals:

Assessment Strategies:

Associated Projects:

Books/Materials Needed:

Bulletin Board Ideas:

Worksheets:

Evaluation of Unit:

_____ Great!   _____ Good   _____ So-So   _____ Never Again!

Comments:

And Then What? — Time to Evaluate

Distinguishing Between Assessment and Evaluation

At the beginning of this book we drew a distinction between the way we have used the terms "assessment" and "evaluation." We have used "assessment" to mean the systematic and purposeful use of various means of gathering and looking at examples of student progress and achievement. "Assessment" presupposes a set of criteria for deciding on the information that is collected. "Evaluation," on the other hand, is used in the sense of judging the collected assessment data and results for one purpose or another. "Evaluation" presupposes a set of criteria by which to judge.

It Used To Be Easy

Assessment used to be easy. You simply gave the tests — usually paper and pencil tests — and collected the data or scores, maybe in the form of percentages. Some students did not test well; people knew that, but that was just the way things were.

Evaluation was just as easy or perhaps even easier. Educators were pretty much sold on the objective, statistical approach to evaluation. This approach was based on the idea of comparison. You (the teacher) compared your students with the scoring tables furnished along with the tests that had been statistically normed on some supposedly representative population of students to see if they (and you) measured up. Or you waited for the newspapers to publish the results that compared your school to others in your district and your district to others in your state.

You also compared one student's progress to the progress of others at the same grade level. "He is working at grade level," you might say to another teacher. "She is reading at 4th grade level," you might report to a parent at conference time. You knew what you meant and so did everyone else.

Finally, you compared each student with the others in your classroom. You might have actually graded on a curve. If not, somewhere in the back of your mind you probably saw a symbolic curve with some people at the top and some at the bottom and a large bump composed of the bulk of the class in the middle of the curve. You saw it this way because this was the way you were taught to see it in a course called something like "Tests and Measurement" that you were required to take in college.

This old view of assessment and evaluation is hard to give up for many reasons, even though we all have had the sneaking suspicion that it did not really tell us everything we wanted to know. One of the main reasons it is hard to give up is the fact that everyone was doing it and everyone understood the premises on which it was based. We had reached a kind of uncomfortable consensus that worked. From kindergarten to college, we could all understand what every other educator was saying. We all know what an "A" student looked like as well as a student who was failing.

And Then What? —
Time to Evaluate *(cont.)*

Why Did Things Change?

People in education gradually began to notice that something was wrong with the way we were assessing and evaluating students. Many factors were considered:

1. The norms on the standardized tests were not in tune with modern, mostly urban, life. They were outdated. They were normed a long time ago when life was simpler. Much of the information called for by the questions was no longer a life experience for students.

2. The norms were not adequate reflections of the population of today. They did not allow for ethnic, cultural, or racial differences or the fact that English might be a student's second language.

3. Studies began to show that while tests may reflect the curriculum, the curriculum also reflects the tests. If you test for minimum proficiencies, teachers begin to teach to minimum proficiencies. Otherwise, really bright students may overshoot the tests.

   For example, if your district's writing sample rubric bases a "Pass" on the ability to write a topic sentence and four supporting sentences, the student who writes a long essay with an implied main idea in response to the prompt may fail the test. In this situation teachers often tell students to write simply and keep it short. The more, and the more creatively, students write, the better chance they have of failing a minimum proficiency test.

4. Tests that compare students are punitive. They sort out what students do not know. They do not allow for individual progress. A student who started out with an "F" on the first test and ended with an "A" on the last test could easily get a "C" for the year's grade if the grades are averaged.

Are Things Getting Better?

Whether or not things are getting better in the areas of assessment and evaluation depends, of course, on what you call "better." Things are definitely less rigid, less objective, less statistical, less secure, more flexible, more subjective, more holistic, more threatening. We are breaking new ground every day and not always sure where we are going.

If you like the new direction of assessment/evaluation, then there are some things you can do to ensure its success. Otherwise, it will go away like other educational innovations that have been poorly understood and implemented in the past. The new performance-based assessment is already on its way out in Great Britain where it was at first whole-heartedly welcomed. Educators there are now saying that it is not rigorous enough and is too expensive to implement effectively.

And Then What? — Time to Evaluate *(cont.)*

What Makes the New Assessment/Evaluation Successful?

The ability to evaluate depends on both the quality and the quantity of the information that has been gathered during the assessment process.

1. So, first of all, there must be enough information. You cannot keep one writing sample in a portfolio and then draw any real conclusion about improvement or progress.

2. The information you gather must be relevant to what you are teaching and the goals you want to achieve. If you are anxious to evaluate the thinking process, you must have information that deals directly with thinking.

3. The information you gather must be significant. While you may teach phonics to young readers as a decoding tool, accumulating information about their knowledge of phonics will not tell you anything at all about their reading comprehension.

Once you have gathered enough relevant, significant information, you will want to look at it in a new and different way.

4. Instead of comparing the information with statistical norms, grade level expectations, or the achievements of others in the class, you will look at the progress made by individual students over a period of time. The fact that you have dated everything in your portfolio system will help you establish a valid time sequence.

5. You will need to convince yourself that subjective evaluation is okay. Your experience and expertise are valid yardsticks with which to measure student progress.

6. You will allow — indeed, you will encourage — students to reflect upon and evaluate their own progress. In this system student awareness and ownership of the learning process is, in itself, an indication of growth.

7. You will welcome parent involvement and input. Parents in many cases see growth that you might miss because they know their children. They certainly see things you might miss in the affective domain. If a student turns in his or her project, you have no idea if the work was independently done, if the student was self-motivated. A parent can tell you things like that.

Worth the Effort

Keeping up with the new trends in assessment and evaluation, trying the strategies, and reading the articles, is really worth it to both you and your students. Even though the whole thing is a real stretch for most of us, just making the effort to implement some of the new ideas will make the classroom into a richer educational environment.

Bibliography

Baskwill, Jane and Paulette Whitman. *Evaluation: Whole Language, Whole Child*. Scholastic. 1988.

Brandt, Ronald S. Editor. *Performance Assessment: Readings From Educational Leadership*. ASCD. 1992.

DeFina, Allan A. *Portfolio Assessment: Getting Started*. Scholastic Professional Books. 1992.

Flood, James and Diane Lapp. "Reporting Reading Progress: A Comparison Portfolio For Parents." *The Reading Teacher*. March, 1989.

Graves, Donald H. and Bonnie S. Sunstein, Editors. *Portfolio Portraits*. Heinemann. 1992.

Harp, Bill. Editor. *Assessment And Evaluation In Whole Language Programs*. Christopher-Gordon Publishers, Inc. 1993.

Hathaway, Walter E. "Toward Expanded Assessment: The Big Picture." (Paper prepared for the 1991 ASCD Fall Mini-Conference)

Herman, Joan L. *A Practical Guide to Alternative Assessment*. Association For Supervision And Curriculum Development. 1992.

Hymes, Donald L. *The Changing Face of Testing and Assessment*. American Association Of School Administrators. 1992.

Kemp, Max. *Watching Children Read And Write*. Heinemann Educational Books, Inc. 1987.

Marzano, Robert J. *A Different Kind Of Classroom*. Association For Supervision And Curriculum Development. 1992.

Meyer, Carol A. *Educational Leadership*. May, 1992.

Moffett, James. *Detecting Growth In Language*. Boynton/Cook Publishers. 1992.

Mullis, Ina V.S. *The NAEP Guide*. The National Assessment Of Educational Progress. April, 1990.

National Research Panel. *Everybody Counts*. National Academy Press. 1989.

Paris, Scott G. "Portfolio Assessment For Young Readers." *The Reading Teacher*. May, 1991.

Paulson, F. Leon, Pearl R. Paulson, and Carol A. Meyer. "What Makes A Portfolio A Portfolio?" *Educational Leadership*. February, 1991.

Perrone, Vito, Editor. *Expanding Student Assessment*. Association For Assessment And Curriculum Development. 1991.

Picciotto, Linda Pierce. *Evaluation: A Team Effort*. Scholastic Canada Ltd. 1992.

Portfolio News. Portfolio Assessment Clearinghouse. Spring 1992.

Portfolio News. Portfolio Assessment Clearinghouse. Summer 1992.

Portfolio News. Portfolio Assessment Clearinghouse. Winter 1992.

Resnick, Lauren B. *Education And Learning To Think*. National Academy Press. 1987.

Rief, Linda. "Finding The Value In Evaluation: Self-Assessment In A Middle School Classroom." *Educational Leadership*. March, 1990.

Sharp, Quality Quinn. *Evaluation: Whole Language Checklists For Evaluating Young Children*. Scholastic, Inc. 1989.

Stiggins, Richard J., Evelyn Rubel, and Edys Quellmalz. *Measuring Thinking Skills In The Classroom*. NEA Professional Library, 1986.

Vavrus, Linda. "Put Portfolios To The Test." *Instructor*. August, 1990.

Wiggins, Grant. "A True Test: Toward More Authentic And Equitable Assessment." *Phi Delta Kappan*. May, 1989.

Wiggins, Grant. *Toward One System Of Education: Assessing To Improve, Not Merely Audit*. Education Commission Of The States. 1991.

Wolf, Dennie Palmer. "Portfolio Assessment: Sampling Student Work." *Educational Leadership*. April, 1989.